# Banishment in the Late Medieval Eastern Netherlands

Edda Frankot

# Banishment in the Late Medieval Eastern Netherlands

## Exile and Redemption in Kampen

palgrave
macmillan

Edda Frankot
Faculty of Social Sciences
Nord University
Bodø, Norway

ISBN 978-3-030-88866-4 ISBN 978-3-030-88867-1 (eBook)
https://doi.org/10.1007/978-3-030-88867-1



This Palgrave Macmillan imprint is published by the registered company Springer Nature Switzerland AG.
The registered company address is: Gewerbestrasse 11, 6330 Cham, Switzerland

# Acknowledgements

My first acquaintance with the Kampen archives came during my PhD, when I was looking for cases of shipwreck, jettison and ship collision. At that time, I only briefly spent time on, arguably, the archives' greatest treasure: the manuscript known as *Digestum Vetus*. As opposed to what its name might suggest, this manuscript has nothing to do with Justinian's laws, but is a fifteenth-century *liber memorialis*, or town book (*stadboek*; *Stadtbuch*). What makes this particular manuscript unique are the more than 200 pen drawings which illustrate many of its entries. Between 2005 and 2006 I became involved in a transcription and digitisation project at the University of Groningen, led by Dick E.H. de Boer in collaboration with Hanno Brand, which sought to make the *Digestum Vetus* and its illustrations more widely available.[1] As such, I became intimately acquainted with its contents. This was the start of my interest in the social and legal aspects of crime and punishment in late medieval Kampen, and I would like to thank Dick and Hanno for setting me on this path, which eventually also led to other transcription and digitisation projects of medieval and early modern sources.

It turned out that there were many more and varied sources available concerning Kampen's legal practice in the second half of the fifteenth century. In the following years I spent many of my free hours trawling through these while being employed on a string of research and teaching jobs. Over time, my focus changed from crime and punishment more generally,

[1] The project was funded by the Dutch Research Council (NWO; file number 380-50-003). The transcription currently remains unpublished.

to sexual offences and morality, to finally settling on banishment. Eventually, the size of the output also grew from one article, via possibly two, to this short monograph. I would like to thank William Hepburn and Frank Jacob for their suggestions to turn a rather long article into two articles and a short monograph respectively.

That I conducted most of the research for this book in my free time and without funding does not mean that there is nobody to thank. First of all, I would like to extend my appreciation to the various members of staff at the Kampen town archives over the years. I was allowed to photograph most of the late medieval archives at various stages, which was a great help when working on this study while living in Dublin, Aberdeen, Rotterdam and Bodø. Most recently, I received assistance from Town Archivist Floris Joustra and Otto Ottens who kindly photographed some final archival pieces, when I was prevented from travelling as a result of the 2020–21 pandemic.

I am also grateful to David Ditchburn and Jackson Armstrong for invitations to disseminate early versions of this research at the Trinity College Dublin Medieval Seminar (2007) and the University of Aberdeen History Seminar (2012) respectively. I would also like to thank the attendees of work-in-progress seminars in Aberdeen (January 2017), especially Jackson Armstrong as the main respondent, and Bodø (February and December 2020) for their comments on earlier drafts of (parts of) this text. Any mistakes, of course, remain my own. I would also like to extend my thanks to my new colleagues in Bodø for extending such a warm welcome in my new home north of the Arctic Circle. Thank you to Sam Stocker and staff at Palgrave for leading me efficiently through the production process and to the anonymous reviewers for their insightful comments. I would also like to thank Nord University's Open Access Fund for financing open access to the book.

Finally, I would like to extend some personal thanks: to my parents Marieke and Herman for continuing to follow my international adventures with enthusiasm, even when it became impossible to meet in person for an extensive amount of time, to Barry for sticking by me despite our many moves, and last, but not least, to Emilia and Scott for being two apples who did not fall too far from the tree. Your enthusiasm for books and many things historic has been an inspiration!

# Contents

# Abbreviations

| | |
|---|---|
| BB | SAK, OA, no. 332 *Burgerboek* (1302–1469) |
| BvR | SAK, OA, no. 5 *Dat Boeck van Rechte dier Stat van Campen* (1313–1416) |
| DN | SAK, RA, no. 242 *Digestum Novum* (1450–1567) |
| DV | SAK, OA, no. 8 *Digestum Vetus* (1448–78) |
| SAK | Stadsarchief Kampen (Town Archives Kampen) |
| GB | SAK, OA, no. 6 *Dat Gulden Boeck* (1329–1614) |
| LC | SAK, RA, no. 2 *Liber Causarum* (1475–1604) |
| LD | SAK, OA, no. 11 *Liber Diversorum C* (1399–1553) |
| LT | SAK, RA, no. 6 *Liber Testium* (1483–93) |
| OA | Oud Archief (Old Archives) |
| RA | Rechterlijk Archief (Judicial Archives) |
| Reg | SAK, RA, no. 1 *Register* (1447–1578) |
| SR | SAK, OA, no. 402 *Stedelijke Rekeningen* (1472–94) |

# List of Figures

CHAPTER 1

# Introduction

**Abstract** This chapter discusses the aims and objectives of the study, a short historiography, a justification of the study's delimitations and the book's structure.

**Keywords** Banishment • (Late) medieval history • Legal history • Kampen • Netherlands

On 3 November 1478 Derick Sael, his wife and their daughter Schele (cross-eyed) Lubbe were sentenced conditionally by the court of the Dutch town of Kampen: they were forbidden to draw or sell any more beer or keep an inn ('herberge holden') in their house. Ignoring this ban would result in their expulsion from the town. It is unclear in what way exactly Derick Sael and his family had offended, but judging by the threat of banishment, it is likely that their house had become a place where immoral behaviour thrived, be it gaming, adultery or prostitution. The phraseology used in the verdict, and in many others which concerned banishment, is meaningful: 'Deden sie dair enthegen soe en wilmen sie hier in der stat niet lijden' ('If they go against this they will no longer be tolerated


E. Frankot, *Banishment in the Late Medieval Eastern Netherlands*,
https://doi.org/10.1007/978-3-030-88867-1_1

in this town').[1] Such language offers important insights into the values of the late medieval Kampen magistrates, values which appear to have been largely shared by the wider population. In fact, 'neighbours' were often the instigators of legal actions against individuals behaving immorally, and they expected the court to take action. The specific legal character of the medieval town as an entity juridically separate from its surroundings meant, moreover, that anyone who would not conform to the town community's legal and moral codes could be ousted from it, either temporarily or for life. The phrase 'soe en wilmen sie in der stat niet lijden' and variations on it are mainly found in cases of immoral behaviour by Kampen inhabitants. Such behaviour consisted of adultery, facilitating prostitution or illegal sexual acts, or generally offensive conduct.[2] In such cases the culprits were either given a warning that they would be banished if they would misbehave again or banished directly.

As will become clear in the following, however, many more people were ousted from Kampen, probably often in absentia, as a result of unpaid fines (and some debts), either because they failed to appear in court or because they were unable to pay these fines. Overall, 26–27 people were banished from Kampen each year. The main aim of this book is to analyse what the practices around the various forms of banishment, but also around the redemption of exiles in Kampen, tell us about the values of late medieval urban society concerning morally acceptable behaviour. Is there, for example, evidence of a similar intolerance towards public debtors or violent offenders as there was towards people displaying immoral behaviour, and is there evidence of a change in value in the second half of the fifteenth century? In addition, this book seeks to show how the town magistrates, in collaboration with the town community, aimed to maintain peace and social order, and to apply authority within Kampen through the

[1] LC, f. 8v (3 November 1478). Other examples: LC, f. 4v (1465); f. 8r (8 Aug 1478); f. 20v (March 1486); f. 26r (23 October 1488); f. 27r (1489); f. 35r (August 1492) (2x); DV, f. 44r (c. March 1461); f. 75v (May 1467).

[2] Prostitution itself was not subject to punishment. Prostitutes were controlled, for example, by placing them under the executioner's supervision (DV, f. 22r (13 January 1456)), but only facilitating it, or procuring, was punished. See also Dupont, *Maagdenverleidsters*, 31, who speaks of the 'moral pragmatism' of the magistrates of late medieval towns. Concerning facilitating illegal sexual acts, see also Helmholz, 'Harboring sexual offenders', 160, who argues that 'from a legal perspective, the important element is allowing the use of premises for immoral purposes'. Money does not need to have exchanged hands to make it illegal. See also Brundage, 'Prostitution in the medieval canon law', for a discussion of canonists' treatment of the issue.

use of banishment and other penal practices. Did these practices, for example, target specific groups in society, is there evidence of public support for them, and did the magistrates utilize rituals and ceremonies to display their power both when banishing and when redeeming offenders?

Banishment was one of the most common punishments in late medieval and early modern Europe. Because of its nature, it also had a lasting impact on medieval society. When exiled individuals were forced to leave their communities, temporarily or permanently removing them from the environment in which they had been causing trouble, society as a whole still had to incorporate these individuals. Removed from their homes, families and social networks, they might be forced into a life on the road, potentially causing even more problems in the town's hinterland, or in other regions and cities. As such, banishment not so much removed the problem, but it moved it or, arguably, made it worse as exiles were potentially pushed into a life of vagabondage or crime.[3] In their turn, the original communities perhaps lost productive members, as well as receiving exiles from other places. Nonetheless, banishment continued to be a popular punishment into the early modern period, especially in the context of urban communities. These communities could police their borders, in the shape of walls, more effectively than other polities.

Yet, despite this ubiquitousness, medieval banishment has so far received relatively little specific attention, especially in English-language publications.[4] The only monograph on the topic, the wide-ranging *Les bannis au Moyen Âge* by Hanna Zaremska (originally written in Polish), was published in 1996. Since then, some valuable case studies have appeared in French and German concerning French, German, Swiss and Polish towns.[5] It will be one of the objectives of this book to make the findings of these studies more widely available. In addition, Napran and Van Houts edited a volume on exile, which focused on elite individuals and their experience of exile, either forced or voluntary between about 900 and 1300.[6] Early modern banishment is better served in the English language. Jason Coy's

[3] Laitinen ('Banishment', 557) points out that urban banishment was not useful from a state perspective.

[4] For a similar observation, see Ewan, 'Crossing borders and boundaries', 239.

[5] Hamel, 'Bannis et bannissement'; Huart, 'Maintenir la paix'; Jacob, 'Bannissement'; Von Brockdorf, 'Die Strafe des Stadverweises'; Hoffmann, 'Der Stadtverweis'; Jeziorski, 'Die Strafe der Ausweisung'; Maurer ('Erzwungene Ferne') and Marchal ('Von der Stadt') both focus on spatial awareness in the context of banishment in medieval Germany and Switzerland.

[6] Napran and Van Houts, *Exile in the Middle Ages*.

book *Strangers and Misfits* analyses in detail the use of banishment by sixteenth-century Ulm magistrates in maintaining public order after the Reformation.[7] Other authors have conducted smaller-scale studies on sixteenth-century Scotland, seventeenth-century Turku and early modern Augsburg.[8] Otherwise, banishment regularly appears in studies on medieval and early modern crime and punishment. In these, the treatment of banishment varies depending on the source material and the aims of the author. Peter Schuster, in his study of late medieval Konstanz, is able to offer a relatively thorough analysis which provided useful comparative material for this study. In Konstanz, like in Kampen, a detailed administration of the financial arrangements between the town and those unable to pay fines is extant.[9] General studies also exist concerning the Low Countries, for example, on Amsterdam, Utrecht and Leiden, as well as a history of medieval criminal law in Flanders by Van Caenegem.[10] A specific study on banishment in the pre-modern Netherlands is, however, lacking. In addition, most studies of banishment focus on exclusion, and much less on inclusion—on gaining re-entry into urban society, which is an important aspect of this study. As such, this book fills two important gaps in research. By focusing almost exclusively on banishment instead of on crime and punishment more generally, this study is also able to offer more detail concerning various aspects of the topic than previous studies.

Most authors agree that banishment is a severe punishment which cuts people from their familiar social environment.[11] Riita Laitinen, for example, stresses that being part of a community was a 'prerequisite for a good life'. In everyday life, honour and reputation were vital, and when these were no longer available because a person was thrown into different surroundings where people did not know them, the results could be

[7] Coy, *Strangers and Misfits*. Coy has also published an article on the topic: 'Beggars at the Gates'.

[8] Ewan, 'Crossing borders and boundaries'; Laitinen, 'Banishment'; Tyler, 'Refugees and Reform'.

[9] Schuster, *Stadt vor Gericht*. Other studies are, for example, Dean, *Crime in Medieval Europe* and *Crime and Justice in Late Medieval Italy*; Burghartz, *Leib, Ehre und Gut* (concerning fourteenth-century Zürich); Næss and Österberg, 'Sanctions, agreements, sufferings' (concerning early modern Scandinavia).

[10] Boomgaard, *Misdaad en straf in Amsterdam*; Berents, *Misdaad in de Middeleeuwen* (also more generally in *Het werk van de vos*); Müller, *Misdaad en straf*; Van Caenegem, *Geschiedenis van het Strafrecht*.

[11] For example, Huart, 'Maintenir la paix', 1.

disastrous.[12] Claude Gauvard, too, stated that when medieval man chose to settle in a place, he would be protected by the ties to parish, church and family that were woven around him.[13] Moreover, as Andreas Blauert has pointed out, a town provided access to legal protection. Being cast out meant that this protection was gone and that exiles were left in relative insecurity and lawlessness.[14] On the other hand, banishments were also easily reversible and in general left people's honour intact. As a result, exiles could reintegrate relatively easily, when provided the opportunity.[15]

Marginalisation has been a hot topic in recent decades, discussing how medieval and early modern communities have excluded different groups from taking part in society fully on the basis of ethnicity, religion, sex or reputation.[16] Reputations might be affected negatively by a person's behaviour or activities, be they professional as in the case of executioners or sex workers, or other, such as criminal. At the same time, the exclusion or rejection of others could form the basis of connections within a community. According to Gauvard, in the preface to Zaremska's book, the functioning of the social body was based on exclusion. By excluding unwanted elements, a community could maintain purity and social peace.[17] Banishment is arguably the epitome of marginalisation.

Zaremska, too, stresses that exclusion is the most radical means by which a community indicates that a person's transgressions are considered severe. This exclusion can be imprisonment, banishment and even death. She points out that social ostracism is well known by sociologists and ethnologists studying small communities, normally originally without the interference of an official justice system. Later, the ostracism usually becomes institutionalised.[18] By studying banishment, then, we can study the type of behaviour that a community or society considered to be so severe that it temporarily or permanently excluded the person guilty of this behaviour.

[12] Laitinen, 'Banishment', 551.

[13] Gauvard in Zaremska, *Les bannis au Moyen Âge*, 7.

[14] Blauert, *Das Urfehdewesen*, 65.

[15] Coy, *Strangers and Misfits*, 111.

[16] See, for example, Hanawalt, 'Rituals of inclusion and exclusion', 18, where she defines marginalisation as 'processes that elevate people in rank and also temporarily or permanently exclude them from their social rank'.

[17] Gauvard in Zaremska, *Les bannis au Moyen Âge*, 9. See also Huart, 'Maintenir la paix', 17.

[18] Zaremska, *Les bannis au Moyen Âge*, 17–21.

Instead of the marginalisation processes within society, this study focuses specifically on the physical exclusion from the community and what this tells us about ideas and perceptions of desired and undesired behaviour. Similarly, the readmittance of exiles can reveal when and why a person might have been considered worthy of redemption. As J. Jeffery Tyler has also usefully concluded, practices of exclusion can show us the social and religious values of an urban community.[19] In contrast to the community in his study (which is post-Reformation Protestant Augsburg), however, the Kampen magistrates and population focused mostly on behaviour, and much less on people's views or beliefs. Both may have sought to eliminate any threats to their civic order and godly society, but following the Reformation the perceived threats to such a godly society had changed from the merely immoral or sinful to the more dangerous heretical. Coy confirms a new post-1550 severity in Ulm as a result of the Reformation, combined with a worsening political and economic situation.[20] In late medieval Kampen, banishment practices reveal certain social norms concerning what was considered moral and immoral behaviour, norms that continued to be prevalent in post-Reformation society, but there is little evidence yet of similar norms regarding ideas and beliefs.

Recent interpretations of the limitations of pre-modern political authority have stressed that public power relied on the collaboration between the governing elite and the rest of society. Lacking a police force and with few public officials, urban authorities were unable to govern or administer justice effectively without the cooperation and consensus of the population.[21] At the same time, courts have been shown to be actively used by the general populace (as 'consumers of justice') to solve their conflicts, or at least to publicize them and their viewpoints in relation to them.[22] Similarly, through denunciation, members of the public could convey their disapproval of the behaviour of their fellows. As Suzannah Lipscomb (studying the Protestant consistory courts of the Languedoc) has already suggested,

[19] Tyler, 'Refugees and reform', 80. See also Hanawalt, 'The limits of community tolerance', 10, for a more general comment on 'community tolerances and intolerances' revealed by the pattern of convictions and punishments.

[20] Coy, *Strangers and Misfits*, 14, 24.

[21] See, for example, Coy, *Strangers and Misfits*, 4–5; Blauert, *Urfehdewesen*, 29; Brakensiek, 'Herrschaftsvermittlung im alten Europa'; Blauert and Schwerhoff, eds, *Mit den Waffen der Justiz*.

[22] Blauert, *Das Urfehdewesen*, 29, referring also to the term 'Justiznutzung' as defined by Martin Dinges. See also Smail, *The Consumption of Justice*, esp. Ch. 5.

through a denunciation a denouncer communicated to others the limits of acceptable behaviour.[23] It was then up to the magistrates to decide whether or not to take action against transgressors or even introduce new regulations. At the same time, denunciations signalled to others in medieval society that certain behaviour was now considered to be undesirable. With this in mind, it would be a misrepresentation to focus on the urban authorities in isolation in this study. Instead, public power is considered taking into account the role of the magistrates and that of the population.

The main focus of this book is Kampen, one of the main trading towns in the northern Netherlands in the later middle ages. It was largely autonomous, administering all justice within its own walls. As a result, it boasts an archive with a wide variety of sources, ranging from civil and criminal court records, and witness testimonies, to various financial records, which together paint a multi-faceted picture of late medieval life, including the legal culture around banishment. Where possible and relevant, this book also offers comparisons with regulations and practices elsewhere in Europe in order to establish to what extent Kampen's practices are representative and to investigate whether or not there was a shared legal culture when it came to banishment. I have chosen to limit myself mostly to the second half of the fifteenth century. This is the earliest period in Kampen history for which a range of sources survives (including the unique *Digestum Vetus* register with its pen drawings, which will be used to illustrate aspects of medieval urban society in this book). Because there is an approximate 10-year gap concerning some of these sources in the final years of the fifteenth and the first years of the sixteenth century, and an exponential rise in available material after that, it makes sense to limit the focus to the period up to about 1500. The second half of the fifteenth century is, moreover, a period of flux when it comes to the perception and treatment of immoral behaviour. Developments in Kampen were part of an urban reform movement which affected many parts of Europe. As such, this book's findings are likely to have relevance more widely. It would be worthwhile to eventually compare the results of the current study with those from a later period, especially as the Reformation started to take effect in the final decades of the sixteenth century, but that is beyond the scope of this book.

The study will firstly set the legal context of banishments in late medieval Kampen by briefly discussing the town's history, administration and

[23] Lipscomb, *Voices of Nîmes*, 151–2.

sources (including the illustrations in the *Digestum Vetus*), before providing an overview of the development of laws and by-laws in the Low Countries in general and Kampen in particular. In Chap. 3, punishment practices in Kampen as a whole are analysed, while banishment as a punitive and coercive measure is the subject of Chap. 4. In this chapter, different aspects of Kampen banishment practices will be discussed. Firstly, the chapter focuses on typologies and quantitative aspects. It will then discuss the question of whether exile was used as a punitive or coercive measure, before moving onto the distance and duration of banishments, and onto the roles of gender and social class, and those of ceremony and symbolism. The final section discusses the question whether or not an 'army of exiles' existed outside of Kampen's walls.[24] Finally, Chap. 5 analyses the practical and ideological issues around the reintegration of exiles into the town community, with a particular focus on the financial arrangements between town and exiles.

[24] Berents, *Misdaad in de Middeleeuwen*, 49, refers to an 'army of exiles' ('leger van ballingen') concerning the town of Utrecht. See also Chap. 4.

CHAPTER 2

# The Legal Context

**Abstract** This chapter gives a brief introduction into late medieval Kampen, the archival sources used in the study, an overview of the historical and legal background of banishment in the Low Countries and a discussion of the by-laws concerning the topic. It also includes a brief description of the images illustrating the contents of one of the manuscripts used, some of which are included in this book.

**Keywords** Local laws • Local administration

## Kampen and Its Sources

In the late middle ages, especially from the mid-thirteenth to the mid-fifteenth century, Kampen was one of the main trading towns in the northern Netherlands, with an estimated population of *c.*6000–8500 in the fifteenth century.[1] A sometimes reluctant member of the Hanse for at least part of this period, the town was situated near the mouth of the River IJssel, which connected the Rhine to the Zuiderzee and the North Sea beyond.[2] As such, Kampen functioned as an entrepot for trade to and

[1] Between 6120 and 8440 according to Van der Vlis, 'De bevolking van Kampen', 14.

[2] Kampen was (re)admitted into the Hanse in 1441, but had shared in the rights and privileges of the Hanse before then and was present at a large number of Hanseatic diets, though less so in the decades directly before 1441. At other times the town did not cooperate with


E. Frankot, *Banishment in the Late Medieval Eastern Netherlands*,
https://doi.org/10.1007/978-3-030-88867-1_2

from the Rhine.[3] In addition, Kampen's ships could be found all the way along northern and western shores, where they transported goods from the Baltic towns to Bruges and further south. In fact, some authors have argued that most 'Kampen' trade took place outside the town itself and that many Kampen skippers (and possibly their ships) only wintered in their hometown.[4] In the second half of the fifteenth century Kampen's position may have stagnated somewhat as a result of competition from merchants and ships from Holland and Zeeland in the transportation between east and west. These towns eventually surpassed the IJssel towns. In 1503, for example, the Sound toll registers show 48 Kampen ships sailing past Elsinore, against 116 from Amsterdam and 331 from Holland.[5] The silting of the IJssel estuary may also have been an issue. But, as will also become clear later,[6] Kampen was still doing well economically in the second half of the fifteenth century, and an actual decline did not occur until the early sixteenth century as a result of conflicts between the dukes of Burgundy/Habsburg and Guelders between 1497 and 1520.[7]

Kampen was situated in the Sticht province in the eastern Netherlands, which was part of the Utrecht diocese, and which included a number of Hanseatic towns with whom Kampen collaborated, such as nearby Zwolle, and Deventer further up the IJssel river. The town had been largely autonomous since the late thirteenth and early fourteenth centuries when it was able to make use of the troubles of its lord, the bishop of Utrecht, to acquire extensive privileges. Important within the context of this study is the privilege granted in 1309, which provided the magistrates with full jurisdiction in legal matters.[8] Thieves, murderers and those that threatened the town's authority could be tried, sentenced and punished in Kampen itself. A few years earlier, in 1302, the bishop had already granted

or even worked against other Hanseatic towns. Weststrate, *In het kielzog van moderne markten*, 40–43; Frankot, *Medieval Maritime Law*, 60–61, and n. 40.

[3] The importance of the Rhenish trade is clear from the amount of 'rijnscippers' (Rhine skippers) mentioned in the sources. In the *Liber Testium*, for example, Rhine skippers appear nineteen times in testimonies concerning criminal cases between 1483 and 1493, referring to ten individuals. LT, ff. 2v, 52v, 72r, 75v, 81r, 116r, 137r, 138r, 141r, 143r, 144r, 200v.

[4] Tamse, 'Economische geschiedenis van Kampen', 213, also referring to Meilink (though without a specific reference).

[5] Tamse, 'Economische geschiedenis van Kampen', 219.

[6] See the openness to immigrants and continuing admission of new citizens in Chap. 5.

[7] Tamse, 'Economische geschiedenis van Kampen', 219, 224, 232, 234, 237; Grooten, 'Kampen an der IJssel', 300–301; Frankot, *Medieval Maritime Law*, 58–61.

[8] Kossmann-Putto, *Kamper schepenacten*, 3–4.

the privilege that Kampen inhabitants could not be tried before a church court in worldly matters. What these worldly matters exactly included was an issue that was contested between the church and urban courts. The traditional church jurisdiction in cases of adultery, perjury, usury and other matters was challenged by the urban authorities relatively early in the Utrecht diocese.[9] Judging by the sources from the second half of the fifteenth century, they appear to have been successful in this challenge. A variety of issues related to marriage were dealt with by the urban courts, as was perjury.

In the later middle ages, the town was governed by 12 aldermen (*schepenen*), supported by 12 councillors (*raden*). The aldermen elected their successors each year (often these were the past year's councillors), while they themselves became councillors. In practice the town was governed by a small group of men, many of whom were members of the rich merchant families.[10] The 'sworn community' (*gesworen ghemeynte*), representing the burghers and consisting of prominent burghers and guild masters, also had a vote in matters of town law and finance. Daily government was conducted by two burgomasters. These were both aldermen and were appointed for a month at a time. These burgomasters also administered justice in the lower court where certain civil cases and fineable offences were dealt with. Appeals and the more serious crimes were handled by the higher court consisting of the aldermen. A higher appeal court consisted of the full board of aldermen and councillors.[11] Originally, a bailiff, as the representative of the bishop, was involved in the administration of justice in capital offences,[12] but there is little evidence of his involvement in the years covered by this study.

A more informal role, that was nonetheless important and confirms the comments made in the introduction on the collaboration between the town magistrates and various groups in society, was played by the 'good men and women'. Most likely, the 'good men and women' were burghers who had a certain standing in society. They are likely to have been married or widowed. They were considered to be honourable and also appear to have been happy to get involved in maintaining social order. The role of the women was perhaps similar to that of the Protestant wives and widows

[9] Kossmann-Putto, 'Stadsbestuur', 61–2; Lange, *Excommunication for Debt*, 212.
[10] Between 1424 and 1500 only 136 individuals were active as aldermen and councillors.
[11] Kossmann-Putto, *Kamper schepenacten*, 4, 5, 7.
[12] Ibid., 8.

of the Languedoc region who positioned themselves as moral guardians by speaking out against immoral behaviour.[13] The 'good men and women' of Kampen appear to have acted as the conscience of the population as a whole and could affect the outcome of a legal case positively or negatively as will become clear in various examples in the following chapters. Over and above that, the population of Kampen can be divided between burghers or citizens and other inhabitants. Access to citizenship rights does not appear to have been very restrictive, though in 1478 it was laid down that new citizens had to be approved by the council.[14] Normally, a fee was also paid.[15] Most craftsmen and merchants would have been burghers. Other inhabitants included recent migrants, servants, marginal individuals like sex workers and others who could not afford the fee.

The Kampen magistrates in the second half of the fifteenth century made use of several registers to record their administration of justice. An important role was played by the town clerk in keeping this administration. With the exception of collections of by-laws and a fourteenth-century *liber memorialis* (the *Oudste Foliant*), legal records are extant from 1447.[16] One of the main sources for information on banishments is the register of 'fugitives and banished outcasts' ('voirtvluchtige & uutgelegde ballinge').[17] This is dedicated mainly to recording people who had fled (and had been declared banished as a result) or those who had been banished because they had been unable to pay their fines. A similar administration had already been kept in the fourteenth century: there is apparently a separate section in the *Oudste Foliant* recording fugitives and banished outcasts,

[13] Lipscomb, *Voices of Nîmes*, 147.

[14] DN, f. 27v.

[15] As far as I am aware, no specific study has been undertaken on the exact rights of Kampen burghers, though it is clear from the regulations in the DN that they included access to certain common areas (e.g. DN, f. 25v (1485)). More generally on citizenship, see Prak, *Citizens without Nations.*

[16] A *liber memorialis* is an urban register (German: *Stadtbuch*; Dutch: *stadboek*) in which town clerks recorded various aspects of government and legal administration which the magistrates considered worthy of remembrance. In fourteenth-century Kampen there were two: the *Oudste Foliant* and its, now lost, predecessor the *Liber Vetus*. Some of the *Oudste Foliant* has been published in Kossmann-Putto, *Kamper schepenacten*. Kossmann-Putto, 'Stadsbestuur van Kampen', 63.

[17] Reg, pp. 78–216 (1447–1578). The register of banishments has been bound in with the register of 'oerveden', the register of capital offenders, the 'jaarkeur' (for all, see below) and 'schadeloos' (warranty against damages).

and it is likely that the book's predecessor included a similar list.[18] The register includes names and offences and, in a majority of cases, the fine due. It may also include the offender's occupation and provenance, a victim (where relevant), the scene of the crime and aggravating circumstances. Such circumstances could be that an offence had taken place at night, which meant a doubling of the fine, or within a designated area of the town, that is to say the area around the town hall, which also resulted in a higher penalty.

There are two extant registers which include actual court cases: the *Digestum Vetus* and the *Liber Causarum*.[19] The *Liber Causarum* runs from 1475 to 1604 and is dedicated to legal cases, criminal, civil and voluntary. A separate register recording capital and corporal offences was set up around 1480.[20] Such offences are also included in the *Digestum Vetus*, a *liber memorialis* dated 1454–73, in addition to other legal cases, by-laws and entries on notable events. The *Digestum Vetus* adds an extra layer of information through the inclusion of a large number of illustrations, which will be discussed in more detail below.

Also relevant is the register of 'oerveden', oaths foreswearing violence to the town, its inhabitants or representatives.[21] These oaths were sworn by people who had spent some time in custody in one of Kampen's prisons, and were often, though not always, also punished by either flogging, the pillory, banishment or mutilation, or a combination of these.

[18] Kossmann-Putto, 'Stadsbestuur van Kampen', 65. I was unable to locate this section in the digital images of part of the manuscript and it was not possible to view the manuscript in person because of travel restrictions.

[19] DV (the first 12 folios have been lost; the *Digestum* also includes entries from 1448, 1453, 1474, 1475, 1476 and 1478)); LC. In this study, the references to the DV use the original foliation. The manuscript was recently renumbered, but I was unable to check the new foliation as a result of travel restrictions.

[20] Reg, pp. 217–310 (1480–1533). As the *Liber Causarum* does not include any capital offences, it is possible that a separate register was already started in 1475.

[21] Reg, p. 1–77 (1477–1568). Similar oaths were common in other parts of Europe, such as the *Urfehden* in Germany. With regard to Germany, see, for example, Boockmann, *Urfehde und ewige Gefangenschaft*, and Blauert, *Das Urfehdewesen*. Blauert differentiates between the 'Hafturfehde', which is the type used in Kampen, and the 'Streiturfehde', which was an older form in which the oath taker foreswore violence against the opposing party. With regard to Germany and the Netherlands (especially Kampen's neighbour Deventer), see: Benders, *Bestuursstructuur*, 155–168. Concerning the older form in France (*asseurement*) and in Scotland (lawburrows) respectively, see Cohen, 'Violence control in late medieval France', 112; G.B. Clark, 'The remedy of lawburrows in Scots law', unpublished LL.M. thesis, University of Edinburgh, 1985, cited by Ewan, 'Disorderly damsels', 158.

Unfortunately, the majority of entries does not include information on the oath taker's crimes. The most important aspect for the magistrates was obviously the fact that someone foreswore violence. A breaking of this oath could result in severe punishment, as is apparent from the case of a man who broke his oath in 1471: Wolter Krauwel was banished from Kampen for life at a distance of ten miles.[22]

An interesting register is that of the 'jaarkeur'.[23] This documents arrangements for the payment of fines in instalments between the town council and individual offenders. Many inhabitants were unable to pay their fines in the first instance, as is also suggested by the fact that people were banished in large numbers for not paying. But the magistrates did offer offenders the opportunity to pay their fine in instalments. In addition, banished inhabitants could arrange (or have arranged for them) a payment plan which would allow them to return to Kampen. Lists of fines are also included in the *Liber Testium* (1483–93) and in the only extant fifteenth-century town account (1472–94).[24] The latter also includes lists of the people who had to pay an instalment of their *jaarkeur* for every year. Overall, the town magistrates kept quite a thorough financial administration of any fines due to them, in addition to a range of legal records.

## The Illustrations in the *Digestum Vetus*

The *Digestum Vetus* provides us with some unique insights into late medieval Kampen society, not only through its contents, but also through a large number of illustrations. These were most likely added by the town clerk, Peter Henricsz, who was appointed around 1444 and who died in 1478.[25] More than 260 pen drawings are included in the manuscript, all of which are related to an element in the accompanying entry. Some show a material object that is relevant to the contents, like a ship accompanying an entry about the freighting of goods to Bergen, or a church tower, a crossbow, a cow and laundry illustrating a by-law proscribing shooting at the church tower and using the cemetery as a meadow or bleaching field (see Fig. 2.1). Others show people, such as a monk when an entry

[22] Reg, p. 12 (1471).

[23] Reg, pp. 372–451 (1465–1514). The *jaarkeur* concerns the payment in annual instalments of fines and debts. A similar administration appears to have existed in Deventer, where it was known as 'jaargeld'. Benders, *Bestuursstructuur*, 171–172.

[24] LC; SR.

[25] De Boer and Frankot, 'Digestum digitaal', 44, 47; Schilder, *Digestum Vetus*, 5–7.

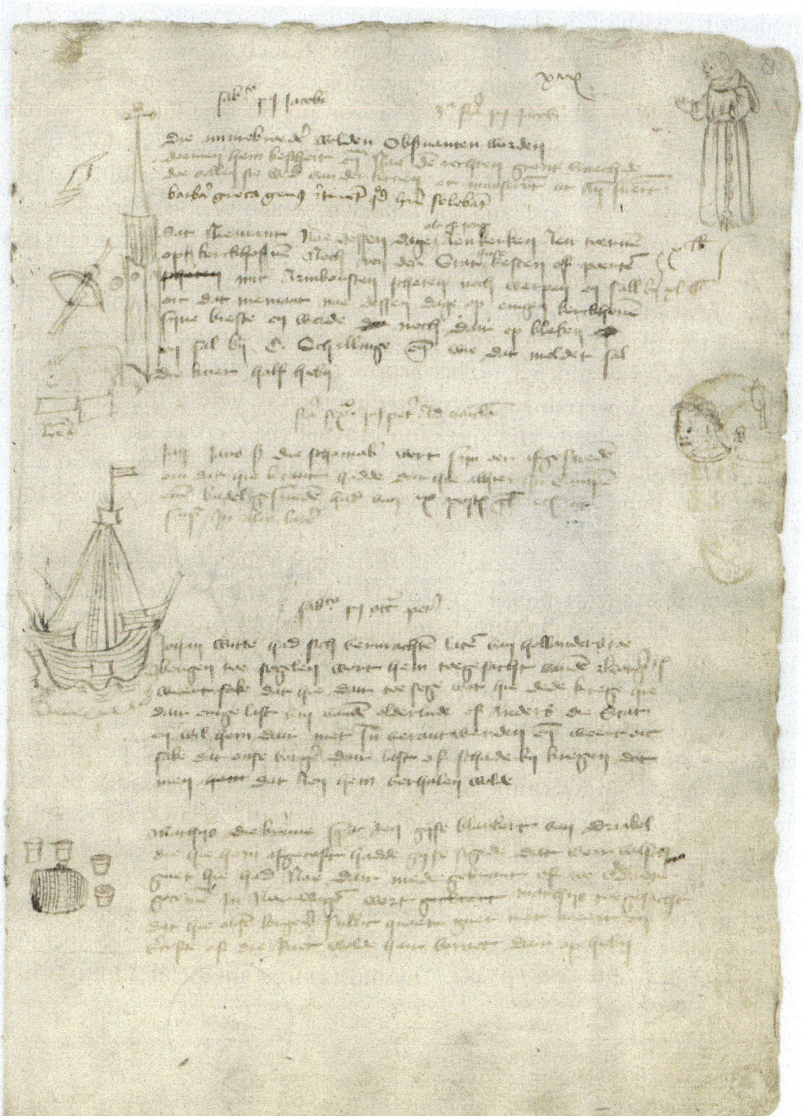

**Fig. 2.1** Example of a full page with illustrations in the *Digestum Vetus* (DV, f. 19r). (© Stadsarchief Kampen, Nederland/© City Archives Kampen, the Netherlands)

discusses the wish of the Franciscans to become Observants (see Fig. 2.1), persons conducting an activity that is discussed, such as brewing, or speeding with their carts, or criminals being subjected to punishment, such as the man who is mutilated by having his ear cut off (see Fig. 2.1), a man being flogged at the pillory (see Fig. 3.3) or a group of people being exposed on the 'kaak', a large pillory (see Fig. 3.1). From the illustrations that we have of the 'kaak' and the pillory at which people were flogged, these appear to have been two separate structures. There are also images of gallows and wheels, mostly drawn quickly and with less detail than most of the illustrations in the manuscript. Highly interesting, finally, are the portraits that have been included illustrating some of the court cases (see e.g. Figs. 4.2, 4.3 and 5.1). These show the defendants, often depicted with their eyes lowered, suggesting their humility before the court. This depiction is more likely an expression of what the clerk considered to be the correct attitude towards appearing before the court, especially in cases of immoral behaviour, than an accurate portrayal of the defendants' demeanour.

The pen drawings are unique in their wide-ranging depiction of late medieval urban life in a legal register. There are a number of possible reasons for their inclusion in this manuscript. Most obviously, Peter Henricsz had creative talent and a love of drawing. Occasional drawings can be found in other late medieval legal registers, but nowhere to this extent. But it most likely also had something to do with the nature of the contents of this manuscript. The *Digestum Vetus* is not the only register that was kept during Henricsz's time, but only this manuscript includes so many drawings. In the *Digestum Novum*, a register of by-laws, for example, there are only seven small drawings.[26] The *Liber Diversorum C* also includes illustrations depicting various objects relevant to the professionals hired by the town council.[27] It is possible that Henricsz was inspired by the contents of the *Digestum Vetus* to such an extent that he included drawings on many of its pages. The illustrations might in addition have

[26] DN, ff. 8r (dice), 8v (cart), 9r (goose), 16r (large pitcher), 21v (dog), 22v (dog), 28v (fish), all drawn during Henricsz lifetime.

[27] I have only seen a small number of pages from this particular manuscript, namely those concerning the executioner (including a sword) and 'stokmeester' (including an image of the stocks), which pages also include entries on the horn blower (with images of horns), the person in charge of the town's guns (with an image of a gun), the bowmaker (including a crossbow) and the harness maker (including a chain mail). It is likely that similar drawings are included elsewhere in this manuscript. LD, ff. 170r, 189r, 195v, 196r, 196v.

assisted in locating particular entries more quickly when information needed to be found. As such, they may have been of practical use as well. In addition, they can be considered to be representations of the urban identity of the magistrates as propagated by the town clerk.[28] In the context of this study, it is useful to analyse the illustrations concerning punishment and the mentioned portraits of miscreants, as these provide an extra layer to our knowledge of the perception of offenders and the representation of public power through punishment.[29] This will be discussed further in the relevant sections below.

## Legal Context

Before turning to the regulations issued by the Kampen town council in the fourteenth and fifteenth centuries, it would be useful to give a brief overview of the historical and theoretical background of banishment in the Low Countries. There is, of old, a difference between banishment (*verbanning*) and outlawry (*vredeloosheid*). An outlaw would lose all rights, and be considered an enemy to society. An exile, on the other hand, was ousted from a territory for a limited or unlimited time and had to swear not to return during that time. The goal of banishment was to remove a person from a specific place where they were considered to be a menace. An exile did not lose any rights and could normally return to enjoy his or her property and business and familial relationships when certain conditions had been met. Another difference between banishment and outlawing was that the former was an actual punishment, whereas the second was a sanction relating to a lawsuit. The accused had broken the rules, either by failing to appear in court or by proving themselves unwilling to be subjected to a punishment. In practice both banishment and outlawing resulted in the exclusion from a community.[30]

According to Van Caenegem, the Old-Flemish laws allowed for temporary or redeemable outlawing. This meant that it was possible for an outlaw to end their exile by appearing in court or paying off a fine or debt. A

[28] De Boer and Frankot, 'Digestum digitaal', 40.

[29] See also the sixteenth-century drawings from Ulm depicting punishments, as discussed by Coy, *Strangers and Misfits*, 130, plus images on 13, 48, 78, 131.

[30] Van Caenegem, *Geschiedenis van het strafrecht*, 137–9, 146. Benders, *Bestuursstructuur*, 177; Napran, 'Introduction', 4. Concerning the early vocabulary of exile and outlawry, see Van Houts, 'Vocabulary of exile'; concerning terminology used in France and England, see also Jacob, 'Bannissement', 1039.

specific practice of banishment appears to have developed within autonomous towns. Banishment was, with fining, the main punishment meted out within the urban jurisdiction of the later middle ages. As a result of the specific organisational and legal form of urban society as a community based (at least principally) on solidarity, freedom and equal rights and duties within a restricted territory, any member of this community who did not cooperate or even actively opposed collaboration was excluded and ejected from it.[31] Van Caenegem differentiates between banishment as the main punishment, as a coercive measure and as an additional punishment. Coercive banishments for the non-payment of fines were a regular occurrence in Flemish towns.[32] Van Caenegem notes the practical similarity to redeemable outlawry. The situation in Kampen appears to have been quite similar to that described by Van Caenegem. Even though the terminology around outlawry (*vredeloosheid*, etc.) was not used in fifteenth-century Kampen for offenders who fled justice (not even those charged with manslaughter), a type of redeemable outlawry whereby an exile could be ended by the payment of a fine seems to have been in use here as well. There is also one example in which a man appears to have been outlawed, although this is not stated explicitly. Johan van Ensz was declared a 'perjurious traitor' ('menedigen verraeder') after having acted against the town and its citizens and broken his *oervede* oath. A bounty was put on his head: anyone who would be able to bring him to justice would receive 100 gold guilders. Dead, he was worth 50 guilders.[33] Banishments were also used as a means of coercion like in the Flemish towns. With regard to manslaughter, offenders were not made wholly lawless. This is different to the practice in Holland and Zeeland in the same period. There, an escaped manslaughterer who did not appear in court on four separate occasions would be outlawed, lost all or part of his goods and could be killed by the victim's relatives with impunity.[34]

With regard to the terminology used in the Kampen sources, there are a few points to stress. The register apparently records 'voirtvluchtige en uutgelegde ballinge': exiles on the run (fugitives) and banished exiles. The terms 'voirtvluchtich' and 'uutgelacht' are subsequently used to describe many of the offenders in the registers, either together or individually. In a

[31] Van Caenegem, *Geschiedenis van het strafrecht*, 154–5.
[32] Ibid., 148, 224–5.
[33] Reg, p. 234 (no date, after 1493). See also LC, f. 37v (1493); Reg, p. 24 (1493).
[34] Glaudemans, *Om die wrake wille*, 170 and table on pages 335–6.

small number of cases other descriptions are used, such as 'die stat verboden' ('banned from the town'). The use of the terms 'voirtvluchtich' and 'uutgelacht', both together and separately, suggests that these were deployed deliberately to differentiate between offenders who fled and those who were banished. This is confirmed by an entry in which only the words 'voirtvluchtig ende' have been deleted, leaving 'uutgelacht'.[35] However, it is difficult to detect the reasoning behind assigning one or the other, or both, in the recorded entries. One would expect a fugitive to also have been declared banished in absentia, but this is not always the case. Also, offenders that are said to have failed to appear in court are sometimes recorded as being banished and at other times as a fugitive and exile.[36] Notable, in this regard, is the entry from 1447 in which a man was declared banished for pulling out a knife, whereas three others were named as fugitives for failing to bring him to court to answer for his offence. Obviously the first man had also chosen not to appear in court, but he was not called 'voirtvluchtich'.[37] Moreover, in 1452 two men had been involved in the wounding of each other. The first was 'voirtvluchtich ende uutgelacht', the second only 'voirtvluchtich'. Both were penalised in the same way for the wounding: they had forfeited a hand or had to pay 200 pounds. It appears then that both were sentenced in absentia. Even the men who had (accidentally) killed someone were variously described as being fugitives or fugitives and exiles. According to a by-law, those guilty of manslaughter were banished until a reconciliation had taken place. It appears, then, that the offenders' status was not always recorded precisely, which suggests that, in practice, fugitives and exiles were considered to have been equal legally.[38] This is confirmed by the use of the word 'balling' for both in some of the relevant by-laws and in the title of the banishment register. For that reason, the terms 'exile' and 'banishment' will be used for both groups. The word 'fugitive', on the other hand, will be used only

[35] Reg, p. 84.

[36] For example, Reg, p. 133.

[37] Reg, p. 79.

[38] This was not the case in the German towns studied by Maurer where, even though both are recorded side by side, a legal differentiation was made between 'Acht' and 'Verfestung' on the one side and 'Verbannung' and 'Verweisung' on the other. Maurer, 'Erzwungene Ferne', 200–201.

to denote those who had fled justice, as some of the by-laws discussed below specifically refer to that group of exiles.[39]

## By-Laws

The Kampen by-laws were recorded mainly in three registers. The *Boeck van Rechte* was compiled in the second half of the fourteenth century, though its oldest dated regulation is from 1313. Its successor, the *Gulden Boeck*, was started in the early fifteenth century.[40] From 1450 new by-laws were recorded every year in the *Digestum Novum*.[41] In 1334 a large number of by-laws were recorded in what are called the 'eerste' and 'andere brieff' (meaning the first and second decree or proclamation), which were copied into the *Gulden Boeck*. These were read out to the population annually to inform them of the communal laws.[42] These decrees stipulated with regard to fines that whoever was unable to pay a fine would be flogged and subsequently banished until the time that the fine was paid. If the fine was as low as 2 lb., a flogging would suffice. This law applied to both burghers and visitors of Kampen. Women would have carried the stone (a yoke with a stone on either side (see Fig. 3.2)) instead of being flogged.[43] It is possible that the flogging was dispensed with at a later time, or was perhaps never executed in practice, as there is no evidence of it being used as an alternative to a 2 lb. fine in the sources from the second half of the fifteenth century. By that time people were banished for failing to pay even these fines.[44]

[39] 'Exile' is here not used in the sense of a banishment, often to a specific place, of a person for political reasons. For this use, see, for example, Van Houts, 'Preface', xi, and Maurer, 'Erzwungene Ferne', 206. Tyler, 'Refugees and reform', 78, points out that one might use 'exile' to denote the expulsion of a citizen, and 'banishment' to indicate that of a non-citizen or foreigner, but that this does not correspond to the terminology used in the sources. He also notes that, linguistically, it has thus far been impossible to differentiate between the various terms used in late medieval and early modern Augsburg with regard to banishment. There, various terms appear to have been used interchangeably.

[40] BvR; GB. Kossmann-Putto, *Kamper schepenacten*, 11; *Overijsselsche Stad-, Dijk- en Markeregten*, vii.

[41] DN.

[42] Kossmann-Putto, 'Stadsbestuur van Kampen', 66.

[43] GB, f. 39v.

[44] For example: Geert Assensoen was banished in 1453 for a fine of 2 lb. resulting from an insult of a woman (Reg, p. 87 (1453)). Similarly, Geertken Walravens was banished for a 2 lb. fine for punching someone in 1464 (Reg, p. 103 (1464)).

In 1352 it was laid down that anyone who fled after a perpetrated offence, be it a breaking of the peace or something else, would be considered guilty of the offence.[45] As such, any fines due for this particular offence would have to be paid before the fugitive would be allowed to re-enter the town. Whoever returned after banishment without authorisation would be due an additional 80 lb. fine, as would those that housed him or her.[46] Half this fine would be meted out to those banished as a result of an unpaid debt.[47] So, although no by-law has survived specifically outlining this, one could also get banished for debts to the city, for example as a result of the lease of property or fishing rights. This is confirmed by some examples in the sources from practice.[48] Fines for illegal return also existed elsewhere, such as in medieval Fritzlar, where the elite was actually meted out a higher fine for a return than the lower social classes.[49]

In the fifteenth century some by-laws were issued with regard to the property of fugitives and exiles. In 1445 it was stipulated, among other things, that when someone fled after a crime, the Kampen magistrates could confiscate any of their goods to pay for the fine. Also, if the offender was renting a property, the owner would be allowed to use anything inside the house to recover the loss of rental payments.[50] To prevent the loss of their goods, exiles most likely tried to remove the contents from their house before these could be confiscated, particularly if they were not intending to return to Kampen. As especially those fleeing from justice would have been in a hurry to leave town, they would generally have needed assistance with this. In 1470 it was laid down in the *Gulden Boeck* that anyone helping fugitives by transporting their household and other goods out of town (either by road or by sea) would risk a fine of 80 lb.[51] In 1477 it was added that any fugitives trying to take away or hide any of their goods from their debtors would lose their citizenship, in addition to

[45] BvR, f. 37v; GB, f. 42r (1352).

[46] Some additional by-laws concerning the unauthorised return to Kampen of exiles are discussed below.

[47] GB, f. 42v (1334).

[48] For example: Tyman Claesz had 'mijnt' (bought by auction) the 'stadswatere', but failed to come up with the full amount. He was banished in 1483 (Reg, p. 130 (1483)). He eventually arranged to pay off his debt in instalments between 1485 and 1492 (Reg, p. 387 (1485)).

[49] Von Brockdorf, 'Die Strafe des Stadtverweises', 47.

[50] GB, f. 105r (18 September 1445).

[51] GB, f. 48v (1446).

a fine of 80 lb. They would be banned from becoming burghers for six years. Anyone assisting them in hiding their goods would be fined 80 lb. Any person looking after any property of the fugitive in their home had to notify the magistrates as soon as they heard about the banishment, on punishment of 80 lb. This property would also be used to pay off any debts.[52]

From these by-laws it becomes clear that fugitives did not lose the rights to their property, though they were not allowed to remove it from the town until any debts were paid. Parts of it could be confiscated. They also did not lose their citizenship. There are no by-laws regulating the property of other exiles, which suggests that they did not lose any rights concerning them and may also have been allowed to take their goods. It appears that all exiles were, in principle, expected to eventually return to Kampen, unless they were, of course, banished for life. In Utrecht, too, exiles could continue to own property in the city, and their goods could be confiscated to offset any damages.[53] The repeated by-laws from the 1470s, banning any help to fugitives, also indicate that they were receiving help from friends and family inside the town after their flight. The same was the case in Holland and Zeeland where exiles were receiving support despite laws proscribing it.[54]

[52] GB, f. 48v (11 December 1477).

[53] Berents, *Misdaad in de Middeleeuwen*, 148–9.

[54] Glaudemans, *Om die wrake wille*, 200.

CHAPTER 3

# Punishment in Late Medieval Kampen

**Abstract** This chapter provides an overview of punishment in late medieval Kampen in order to provide a context for the use of banishment. It discusses various punishments utilised in Kampen, such as symbolic, shameful, corporal and capital punishments, fines and imprisonment, as well as some of the town's officials involved in punishment.

**Keywords** Punishment • Crime

The number of by-laws recorded in the Kampen sources suggest that banishment played a significant role in the town's legal practice. This is confirmed by many of the other extant sources. But before we quantify and qualify banishment as a punitive and coercive measure, it would be useful to consider it in the context of punishment in late medieval Kampen as a whole.

It is difficult to get a complete overview of punishment, as relevant information is spread out across a number of sources, and these sources differ in character and purpose, as well as covering different periods. It is especially difficult to get an overview of the fines and what they were imposed for.[1] As such, there is little point in trying to quantify precisely

[1] Fines were recorded in different registers: the town accounts (1472–94) include lists of fines, but especially for the earlier years these do not specify what the fines were imposed for. The *Liber Testium* (1483–93) includes similar lists. A sample check of the lists in these two sources for 1490 shows that these overlap, but not fully. For example, in the town accounts


E. Frankot, *Banishment in the Late Medieval Eastern Netherlands*,
https://doi.org/10.1007/978-3-030-88867-1_3

how often specific punishments were imposed in Kampen in this period. It is possible, however, to sketch more broadly the different types of punishment and indicate their approximate use (in as far as they appear in the extant sources) in comparison to that of banishment.

It is clear that the most common punishment that was imposed by the Kampen courts was a fine. This was the same in most places in Europe at this time.[2] Fines were paid to make amends for wrongs done to victims, a chance for the culprit to redeem themselves and become a full member of the community again. This corresponds to the original meaning of the Germanic words for fine (*Buße*, *boete*): an amendment, also used in religious contexts as an atonement or penance.[3] In fourteenth-century Zürich, for example, there were two different kinds of amends: one to the city (*Stadtbuße*) and one to the victim (*Klagerbuße*).[4] In Kampen, fines could range from 2 lb. for small offences, such as insult, to 200 lb. for woundings that had taken place at night.[5] Violent offences especially, if they did not result in death, were punished by imposing fines. These fines are detailed in the Kampen by-laws and appear to have been strictly enforced by the lower court, as will become clear below. The same offence

there are 194 entries (ff. 181v-183v), in the *Liber Testium* 264 (ff. 143r-144r and 160r-161v). Missing from the accounts are mainly the entries of the offenders who were banished (and were therefore transferred to the banishment register) and a list of 21 people fined for 'struuc' (offal?) and 'drec' (dirt). A small number from the accounts is missing in the *Liber Testium*. Information on (initially) unpaid fines is recorded in the 'jaarkeur' register, the banishment register and the 'jaarkeur' section in the town accounts.

[2] Concerning fines as the dominant form of punishment—regularly on a par with banishment with regard to frequency—in the middle ages and early modern period, see, for example, Dean, *Crime in Medieval Europe*, 130–4 (also quoting Robert Muchembled's *Les temps des supplices: de l'obéissance sous les rois absolus, XVe-XVIIIe siècle* (Paris 1992), 28, 39, 48, 82); Berents, *Het werk van de vos*, 190; Müller, *Misdaad en straf*, 118; Boomgaard, *Misdaad en straf in Amsterdam*, 160; Laitinen, 'Banishment', 551; Næss and Österberg, 'Sanctions, agreements, sufferings', 146; Burghartz, *Leib, Ehre und Gut*, 87 (concerning Zürich), noting, however, that in other places like Basel, banishment was the primary punishment that could be bought off with money.

[3] 'Boete—((geld)straf)', Nicoline van der Sijs, *Etymologiebank* (2010). Available at http://etymologiebank.ivdnt.org/trefwoord/boete (accessed 13 May 2021).

[4] Burghartz, *Leib, Ehre und Gut*, 87; Zaremska, *Les bannis au Moyen Âge*, 69.

[5] The Kampen registers refer to a number of currencies, but fines are most commonly stated in pounds. However, there is a differentiation between 'town's pounds' (*stat* lb., in earlier manuscripts just 'lb.') and 'lord's pounds' (*hern* lb.). The latter were worth four times as much as the former. Towards the late fifteenth century, amounts in the legal registers are stated increasingly in *hern* lb. In this book lb. and pound indicate *stat* lb., unless otherwise indicated.

would receive the same fine every time, irrespective of the social status of the offender or the victim.[6] As mentioned in Chap. 2, the fine would be doubled when there were certain aggravating circumstances. Charging equal fines for equal crimes on first inspection gives the impression of a fair system. But as Zaremska justly points out, it is only fair to those who could actually afford to pay the fine.[7] Culprits who could not afford it received additional punishments, such as banishments. Fines were mostly imposed by the lower court of burgomasters and only very occasionally by the higher court, judging by the sources regarding its business. There is no evidence that the victims were compensated for any kind of crime, such as was the case in Zürich in the fourteenth century. By that time, the development from a system of amends made to victims to one of fines paid to the administration had apparently come to a conclusion. The town was amended for a breaking of the peace and the culprit was punished.[8]

Other punishments appear more regularly in the records of the higher court. This court had a great variety of measures at its disposal and appears to have been more flexible than the lower court in imposing these. In its verdicts, the court seems to have taken into account personal circumstances, though it is often unclear what these were. This will be discussed further below. In addition to having a range of punishments at its disposal, the court also made use of its discretion in merely giving a warning to an offender which often included the threat of a future punishment. In fact, warnings make up about half of the measures imposed in the *Liber Causarum* between 1474 and 1500. They account for a slightly lower share in the *Digestum Vetus* in the third quarter of the fifteenth century. This lower share can be attributed to the fact that the *Digestum Vetus* also records cases which resulted in capital or corporal punishments, whereas the *Liber Causarum* does not. The warnings given to offenders could include the threat of a wide range of punishments, such as banishment, imprisonment, shameful punishment or a loss of rights. Often it also included vaguer descriptions, most commonly that offenders would be made an example of ('dat sich dair een ander exempel aen nemen sall').[9]

The next most common punishment in the *Liber Causarum* and *Digestum Vetus* (not counting capital punishment) was banishment, which

[6] See, for example, the fine for wounding a 'guest', Reg, p. 112 (1469).
[7] Zaremska, *Les bannis au Moyen Âge*, 70.
[8] Ibid., 73.
[9] For example, DV, f. 30v (27 June 1458).

was imposed in about one in six cases in these registers.[10] Another punishment which was handed out regularly was the loss of rights. This could range from a ban on exercising a certain profession or particular tasks, to being declared dishonourable (and as such unable to act as witness) or 'onmondig' (incapable of self-government), to losing one's burgher rights. For example, Dyrck Selle, a barber, in 1484 was forbidden to conduct any more bloodletting, since people had died or had become 'lame', confirming to the court that he was not competent in bloodletting ('wair wt blijket dat hie vant laten ghien verstant en hefft'). He was also banned from barbering and shaving on Sundays.[11] In 1495 Ghyse Koperslager lost his burgher rights as a result of ignoring written orders to appear in court. The court stated that he would not be able to regain these rights, but just over a year later a settlement had apparently been reached and Ghyse was given back his burgher rights after all.[12]

Though monetary fines were only occasionally imposed in the higher court, a more regular type of punishment meted out was a fine payable in stones. These stones could be utilised for the building and maintaining of public works such as the town wall. A fine in stones also appears to have had a more symbolic function, in that an offender could be considered to contribute to the common good more directly than when simply paying in coin. In addition, fines in stones were sometimes imposed on offenders who had requested to be granted mercy instead of a punishment. For example, in 1486 Geertken Schele was convicted of dishonourable behaviour. She was granted mercy, although the court stated that she actually deserved a harsher correction ('scarper correctie'). She had to contribute 80,000 stones to the common good, a relatively large amount.[13]

Other punishments also had a decidedly symbolic purpose in that offenders had to publicly show their humility and right the wrong which they had committed, either by asking a pardon, by taking back words or by taking part in a church procession. The latter meant that the offender had to appear bareheaded and barefooted, usually carrying a wax candle of a certain weight. Such processions of humble offenders were not particular to Kampen—they have been recorded in many places, such as

[10] Hoffmann ('Der Stadverweis', 197) also states that banishment was one of the main punishments in medieval town laws.

[11] LC, f. 25v (18 May 1484).

[12] LC, f. 41r (19 March 1495).

[13] LC, f. 20v.

Aberdeen.[14] This common legal culture can no doubt be linked to the influence of the Church and its practices of repentance. In Kampen, in 1485, Rolof Zwarte and his wife were convicted of 'kwade herberg' ('bad inn'—facilitating prostitution). They received a fine of 15,000 stones. If they were unable to afford this, their alternative punishment was to walk in front of the church procession with bare feet and a bare head carrying a burning candle weighing half a pound on six Sundays: on three occasions they had to walk around St Nicholas church yard and on three other occasions around St Mary's churchyard.[15] This way, their public penance would be witnessed by the members of the two main parishes of the town.

Insults usually incurred a fine, but at times they had to be renounced by the offenders. In 1493 Henrick Gosensz had to stand on the 'callebanck' ('callen' meaning to talk or to tell, but also to babble or talk nonsense) and 'swallow' the words he had spoken against Reyner Warnbolsz.[16] At other times, especially when an official had been insulted, offenders were made to ask forgiveness, such as in the case of Dirck Kerchoff who had displayed a 'drysten onhoeftschen mont' ('bold and discourteous mouth') when speaking about a burgomaster. He was made to ask the whole council for forgiveness while bareheaded.[17] A more extensive procedure was recorded when Dyrck van Allenkerken had insulted the wife of Johan Wenemersz in 1486. This was considered to have been such an attack on her reputation that witnesses ('gueder manne ende vrouwen') had been called in and that Dyrck was sentenced to doing a public penance. Firstly, he had to repeat a lengthy statement, before he had to take part in three church processions. In addition, Dyrck would be declared dishonourable. In the end, the sentence was not read out to Dyrck, because he fled before he could receive it. Apparently, he sought sanctuary in the Broederkerk, one of the churches

[14] For example, on 16 January 1476, two men were convicted of 'strublans' and 'strublans and hurting' respectively: Davy Crukschank who had to ask the baillies for forgiveness in a loose gown, bareheaded and carrying a pound of wax, during mass at Saint Nicholas church, and Adam Walker who had to walk before the procession with bare feet, legs and head, carrying a candle weighing a pound in one hand and a knife in the other, the latter of which he had to offer to the baillies, while also asking their forgiveness. Frankot, et al., eds, *Aberdeen Registers Online*, ARO-6-0416-01 (accessed 1 November 2020).

[15] LC, f. 19v.

[16] LC, f. 38r. For similar practices involving the utterance of the words 'tongue you lied', see Ewan, 'Tongue you lied'.

[17] LC, f. 38r.

in Kampen, which is unusual considering he was unlikely to receive a corporal punishment.[18]

The interesting thing about this case is that the statement was recorded in the register. It presents us with a clear message about the importance of reputation in late medieval society:

> All the dishonourable words which I have told or spoken secretly or publicly in any way concerning Johan Wenemersz' housewife, I have altogether made up and they are false and untrue [more words about the false nature of what he had said] and I 'cloppe' these words altogether in my mouth once, twice, three times, and confess that I have acted like a crook, as I only know her to be a good woman. And furthermore, I pray to the honourable council of Kampen, the aforesaid woman, and all her friends, men, and women, that they will forgive me, and that they will hold and consider those words to have been false and untrue.[19]

Renouncing words, asking for forgiveness and other such measures had a number of functions: first of all, the offended party was offered, in public, a symbolic compensation for a slight, but also an opportunity to showcase their generosity and mercy. The offender had to show humility publicly, and to admit their wrongdoing, but they were also offered a way to be reconciled with the person offended and the town community more

[18] The Broederkerk was apparently used more often as a place of sanctuary: in 1540 Herman Glasemaker sought sanctuary there after a manslaughter, but he was taken away from there and put into prison on suspected murder. He was later returned to the church after it had been decided that it had not been murder. A similar thing happened some weeks later with Cristoffer van Coesvelt. Reg, p. 41 (May/24 July 1540). It appears, then, that by this time sanctuary did not fully protect an offender, especially in the most serious cases, like murder.

[19] 'Alle die oneerlyke woirde die ick in enigerwijs van Johan Wenemerssz huysfrouwe heymelick off openbair gekalt ende gesproken hebbe, die hebbe jick altoesamende versiert ende synt logentalich ende onwairachtich ende hebbe dair noch well noch wair angesecht mer hebbe oir sodane woirden quellyken ende valschlyken als een bove over versiert ende gelogen ende myt logentaell over bedichtet ende overgesecht. Ende cloppe die altoesamende in mijnen mont ene werve, ander werve, ende derde werve, ende bekenne dat ick dair niet well noch wair mer als een schalck an gedaen hebbe, want ick van hair anders niet en weet dan van ene guede vrouwe. Ende bidde voirt den erbaeren raet van Campen, der vrouwen voirs., ende alle oeren vrenden mannen ende vrouwen dat sie mij dyt omme die mynne van gode wyllen vergeven, ende sodane woirden voirt voir logende ende onwairachtich holden ende achten wyllen.'—LC, f. 21v.

generally.[20] Taken together, such symbolic punishments were also reasonably common.

Of a slightly different character were shameful punishments, which were equally public but entailed a more unpleasant psychological and, at times, physical experience for the offender. The 'kaak', a type of pillory, features regularly in legal language, but its use was less common in practice than the references in by-laws and warnings suggest. Only one person was punished by being made to spend time on the 'kaak' directly according to the verdicts in the *Liber Causarum* and the *Digestum Vetus*.[21] This is contrary to the scene depicted in the *Digestum Vetus*, where the platform at the top of the pillory appears rather crowded (see Fig. 3.1), with three (nearly) nude offenders on display. An official appears to be on his way down from the ladder. This illustration accompanies a by-law about adultery, and seems to be rather a representation of public power than a depiction of an actual situation. The 'kaak' features in the *oerveden* register more regularly, as does carrying the stone, a punishment mainly for women (see Fig. 3.2).[22] In the meantime, when not used, pillories stood on medieval market squares throughout Europe as symbols of political power. On the rare occasion that shameful punishments were imposed, the impact on the culprit could vary depending on social status. Those with more of a reputation to uphold were likely to be damaged more than a person with a low status from outside of town. As a result, magistrates probably also had less scruples using shameful punishments on the latter group.[23] The impact of shameful punishments could be increased by the staging of different aspects of it. The culprits could be forced to walk through town wearing ridiculous clothing, or be presented naked or in their underwear. They could be made to carry silly or symbolic attributes and be accompanied by sounds that attracted attention (bells, drums, pipes, etc.).[24] The shame of being displayed on a high pillar in the square by the town hall without one's clothes as markers of social

[20] Dean, *Crime in Medieval Europe*, 134 (more generally about 'corrective penalties': Ewan, 'Crossing borders and boundaries', p. 247).

[21] DV, f. 44v.

[22] For example, 'kaak': Reg, p. 6 (1459; 1462), p. 14 (1477), p. 15 (1478); stone: Reg, p. 16 (1480), p. 20 (1486), p. 21 (1489). Concerning this punishment elsewhere, see De Win, 'De schandstraffen', 41–73.

[23] Schwerhoff, 'Verordnete Schande?', 158, 172, 174, 176. Schwerhoff also points out that there is a differentiation in German between 'Schandstrafe' and 'Ehrenstrafe', but that this difference is not clear in legal practice.

[24] De Win, 'De schandstraffen', 34, 55.

**Fig. 3.1** The 'kaak' (DV, f. 21v (20 December 1455)). (© Stadsarchief Kampen, Nederland/© City Archives Kampen, the Netherlands)

status is apparent in the image of the 'kaak' in the *Digestum Vetus*.[25] There are no details of the practice of carrying the stone in Kampen and the illustration is not particularly informative in that regard, despite the fact that it accompanies an entry in which a woman is sentenced to carrying the stone for perjury.[26] In medieval Flanders, some stones and details about them and

[25] See also Hanawalt, 'Rituals of inclusion and exclusion', 27, on the importance of clothing in boundary enforcement.

[26] DV, f. 50r (18 October 1462).

**Fig. 3.2** The 'stone' (DV, f. 50r (18 October 1462)). (© Stadsarchief Kampen, Nederland/© City Archives Kampen, the Netherlands)

their use have survived. They were quite heavy, for example: surviving stones from Damme weigh 6 kg each, and elsewhere they were laid down to be 9 kg a piece. Offenders had to walk a significant distance with them accompanied by officials and others. In the by-law of Dorialmé, wearing padding or protective clothing was proscribed.[27] Whether or not the practice was entirely the same in Kampen, we can assume that carrying the stone should also be considered to have been a corporal punishment there.

Corporal punishments, in the strict sense of inflicting punishment on the body of an offender directly,[28] are found in the *Digestum Vetus*, but not in the *Liber Causarum*. This may be because, by the time the *Liber Causarum* was instituted in 1475, such punishments had started to be registered separately. A specific register recording corporal and capital punishments is extant from 1480, but it may have had a predecessor. Some corporal punishments were also included in the *oerveden* register.

[27] De Win, 'De schandstraffen', 51.

[28] For the argument that 'few punishments are not corporal', see Geltner, *Flogging Others*, 21–5.

Unfortunately, this register does not record all of the punishments already inflicted on the lawbreakers who were made to swear an oath. So, there may have been more. The image that arises from these sources concerning corporal punishment in Kampen is that these were not imposed very regularly. Floggings were the most common. Such floggings can also be considered shameful punishments, as they were generally conducted in public, such as at a pillory (see also Fig. 3.3).[29] In addition, as Trevor Dean has pointed out, it 'carried associations with penances imposed for sin', as public whippings were also imposed by church courts.[30] Once every few years an offender lost an ear (or part of it) or an arm, or was branded.[31]

**Fig. 3.3** Offender being flogged at the pillory (DV, f. 16v (24 April 1455)). (© Stadsarchief Kampen, Nederland/© City Archives Kampen, the Netherlands)

[29] An exception are the two floggings that were conducted in prison, one of them specifically to lessen the shame ('om der mynste scande willen'). Reg, p. 25 (1500); p. 27 (1501).

[30] Dean, *Crime in Medieval Europe*, p. 134.

[31] For example, ear: Reg, p. 5 (1455); DV, f. 45av and Reg, p. 9 (1467); Reg, p. 12 (1471); p. 13 (1475); p. 15 (1477); p. 16 (1480, twice); p. 17 (1482); branding: Reg, p. 4 (1453); p. 7 (1464, three men); p. 8 (1464); p. 8 (1466); p. 14 (1477).

There is a single example of a man's eyes being gouged out after he had been convicted of being involved with preventing Kampen merchants from reaching the Antwerp market in 1495.[32] Such mutilations also had a decidedly shameful aspect to it, as they were inflicted to mark offenders as dishonourable for life. In some cases, mutilation was imposed as a merciful punishment: around 1467, Johan, the son of Jan Melijsz, was convicted of general misbehaviour and a number of small thefts, a crime normally punishable by death. Because the 'good women of the town', Johan's father and his guild prayed the court for mercy, however, only his ear would be cut off.[33]

Even though the Kampen higher court can be seen to have given out warnings and suspended punishments very regularly and, as such, could be considered to have been relatively mild towards its offenders, it can also be seen to act very harshly against the most serious offenders, and on a reasonably regular basis. There is a record of 73 executions between 1455 and 1500, but it is doubtful whether this record is complete. The *Digestum Vetus* includes 29 executions, between zero and four per year. The record runs until 1473, but there are two additional executions from 1475 and 1476 respectively. The register of corporal and capital punishments starts in 1480, but is somewhat chaotic when it comes to its chronology. In addition, there were significantly more executions recorded in the first years, when the record does appear in a largely chronological order. As such, it is unclear whether the register offers a full picture of mutilations and executions from 1480 onwards. On the other hand, because they were such memorable occurrences, it is quite likely that most executions were recorded. It may well be that there were simply no executions in some years.[34] Overall, the register records 44 executions, between zero and seven per annum, but between three and seven in the years from 1480 to 1485.

These do not appear to be very high numbers, but in fact, in the *Digestum Vetus*, more people are recorded to have been sentenced to death than to banishment. Also, when comparing these numbers to those in other Dutch towns for which records exist, the annual average is slightly

[32] Reg, p. 307 (6 September 1495); Reg, p. 25 (*oervede*).

[33] DV, f. 45av; Reg, p. 9 (1467).

[34] The record after 1500 appears to be better organised, but there too there are years without any recorded executions, such as 1501, 1503, 1504, 1505, 1506, 1509, 1513, 1514, 1519. Reg, pp. 248–304.

higher than elsewhere. In Amsterdam between 1524 and 1552, 186 persons were executed (c. 6.6 per annum), but 61 of these were Anabaptists executed in 1535. Discounting these 61, the annual average is 4.4 in a city which grew from c. 11,500 inhabitants in 1514 to 27,000 in 1560 and, as such, was 1.5–3 times larger than Kampen.[35] In Utrecht (c. 20,000 inhabitants) 57 people were put to death between 1426 and 1455, less than 2 per annum.[36] In Haarlem (which grew from c. 8000 inhabitants in 1400 to 16,000 in 1550) the average was 2.2 per annum in the second half of the fifteenth century.[37] The image of relative harshness is exacerbated by the fact that, in nearly half of the cases in the *Digestum Vetus*, punishments of hanging or beheading were combined with drawing and/or being broken or displayed on the wheel. It is clear that the Kampen magistrates used these executions as opportunities to display their power and commitment to maintaining public order. Those convicted tended to be men from outside of town who had confessed (most likely under torture) to a number of thefts or robberies and other serious crimes, such as murder, in different locations (see also Chap. 4). An extreme case was that of Hans Karstgensz who, in 1486, was convicted of not only a long list of thefts and some murders, but also rape and bestiality. He was drawn and burned.[38] No other living person was burned in the second half of the fifteenth century, though a woman had originally been sentenced to burning for infanticide. She was granted mercy and was beheaded instead. Her corpse was burned and buried in a hole.[39] The body of the only suicide case in this period was also burned.[40] So the Kampen magistrates appear to have had no qualms about treating these men (and the occasional woman), who generally had no connection to the community, or those whose behaviour or ideas were perceived to pose a very serious threat to this community, harshly. Citizens of Kampen, on the other hand, were likely to be treated more leniently, or to be granted acts of mercy, like the lady convicted of infanticide, or the

[35] Boomgaard, *Misdaad en straf in Amsterdam*, 182–3.

[36] Berents, *Misdaad in de Middeleeuwen*, 38.

[37] Müller, *Misdaad en straf*, 40, 65 note 94, 88.

[38] Reg, p. 231 (January 1486).

[39] Reg, p. 243 (21 May 1492). There are a few more cases of burning in the first half of the sixteenth century. All of the living had been convicted of bestiality, and another suicide victim's body was also burned. Reg, p. 271 (1512), p. 275 (1516), p. 281–2 (1520); p. 290 (1530). Three female Anabaptists in 1544 were drowned by putting them in a sack and throwing them in the IJssel river. Reg, p. 304 (1544).

[40] DV, f. 19v (8 August 1455).

men and women who were mutilated, flogged or made to suffer demeaning rituals instead of being executed, like Johan, Jan Melijsz's son mentioned before.

A final punishment that should be considered is imprisonment. As has been pointed out elsewhere, punitive imprisonment did exist in the middle ages, but it was used sparsely.[41] This was partly due to the limited capacity of medieval prisons. Instead, prisons were used to confine individuals awaiting trial and for short imprisonments.[42] In England and Italy, among other places, debtors (including those with public debts and unpaid fines) were imprisoned. These imprisonments, though supposedly coercive, also had an important punitive aspect to them.[43] For poor debtors, rising fines became increasingly impossible to pay back, especially without access to work, resulting in practically indefinite imprisonments of which the coercive value can be questioned.[44] The development of the prison systems in the Italian city states is part of a centralisation and institutionalisation of power that had not yet taken shape in the northern Netherlands to the same extent in the later fifteenth century.[45] In addition, Kampen was a relatively small autonomous town that did not have the capacity to house and maintain a large number of prisoners at any one time. But punitive imprisonment was being practised in Kampen and there were a number of locations in the town where potential offenders could be locked up for short periods of time. The 'Wiltvank' or 'Wiltgang' is named a few times and was probably the most used.[46] It was also the location where suspects could be tortured. This was true for the seventeenth century and appears to have been for the early sixteenth century too, when two women were imprisoned there to be subjected to torture.[47]

That imprisonment was also used as a punishment in Kampen is suggested by a couple of by-laws. In a (later deleted) by-law from 1404, it was

[41] See, for example, Carrell, 'The ideology of punishment', 312; Blauert, *Das Urfehdewesen*, 59–60.

[42] Berents, *Misdaad in de Middeleeuwen*, 43–7; Dean, *Crime in Medieval Europe*, 120–4.

[43] Ireland, 'Theory and practice', 57; Geltner, *The Medieval Prison*, 44–54. See also further below.

[44] Geltner, *The Medieval Prison*, 47, 59, 101.

[45] Ibid., 130. In addition, the development of prisons also fits into the development of a wider Western European 'persecuting mentality' in the later middle ages and in the change from excluding marginals to including them, though within bounds. Geltner, *The Medieval Prison*, 103–6.

[46] Van Vliet, 'Kamper Scherprechters', 89.

[47] Ibid.; Reg, p. 272 (1515).

laid down that people who allowed dice games to be played in their home should pay a fine in addition to a month 'opten Wiltganghe'.[48] This by-law appears to replace another from 1388 according to which someone who allowed such games would be locked in 'a tower' with his family for 14 days, living on bread and water.[49] The use of imprisonment as a punishment is confirmed by cases from legal practice. In 1461, Hendrik van Groningen, who had been charged with a variety of offences including domestic violence and adultery, was given a warning that if he continued his behaviour, he would be put in the 'Wiltfang' in addition to being subjected to another, undefined, punishment which would act as an example.[50] His reputation as a philanderer is confirmed by the drawing illustrating the entry (see Fig. 3.4), where he can be seen entangled with a lady in an outdoor setting. His hat is lying by their side. This image provides a stark contrast with others (e.g. see Figs. 4.2, 4.3 and 5.1) in which the accused are not depicted in compromising situations. It seems that the clerk had a particularly low opinion of Hendrik van Groningen. In 1501, Beerte Bastz, a man convicted of bad dealings as a merchant ('valse comenschap'), was imprisoned in the Hagenpoort, one of the town's gates, for a 'long time'.[51] Unfortunately, it is not specified how long exactly, but it is

**Fig. 3.4** Hendrik van Groningen (DV, f. 42r (24 January 1461)). (© Stadsarchief Kampen, Nederland/© City Archives Kampen, the Netherlands)

[48] BvR, f. 40r.

[49] BvR, f. 36r (1388).

[50] DV, f. 42r (24 January 1461). It appears that Hendrik was eventually banished, as another man was convicted for helping Hendrik remove his goods in 1462 (Reg, p. 101).

[51] Reg, p. 27 (1501). The Hageninger gatehouse also functioned as the official residence of the 'stokmeester'. LD, f. 218v (c. 1468). The location was not specifically named in 1432, LD, f. 170r.

unlikely to have been years. As evidence from elsewhere suggests, prison sentences tended to be short in late medieval Europe.[52]

Other prisons that are mentioned are the 'Wulentoerne', which was one of the town's towers, and the 'Merehuus'. As a punishment for knocking a couple of teeth out of someone's mouth, a man simply know as 'Jelle' was put in the 'Wulentoerne' for an undefined amount of time.[53] In 1471, Jutte van Bronnepe was convicted of facilitating prostitution and speaking immorally. She was banished and warned that she would be brought to the 'Merehuus' before being banished if she would not leave of her own accord.[54] It is unclear where or what the 'Merehuus' was. If Jutte would return to Kampen, she would be held in town custody while the court considered her punishment. It is clear that the judges wanted to ensure that Jutte left Kampen never to return. A 'schamel jonck wijfken' ('humble young woman'), identified as 'Swarte [Black] Geertken' in another source, finally, was sent to Utrecht to spend the rest of her days in a closed convent after she had been caught up in undefined youthful foolishness.[55] The Koornmarktspoort, one of the other gates, could also be used to lock people up, as is clear from the employment brief of the man put in charge of keeping the town's guns. His official residence was at the gate, and he was also expected to take care of any prisoners when relevant.[56]

In general, when it comes to imprisonment, though, there is no mention of a specific location and individuals were said to have been 'in prison' or 'imprisoned' ('in hachte', 'in den stocke', 'in vangenisse' or 'gevangen'). All the offenders who had to swear an oath had been in 'stat hachte' for various offences and were only released on swearing an oath that they would do no further harm. In fact, the standard oath, which is recorded at the start of the register, includes the words 'om des wil dat ic in der stat hachten ende vengnisse geseten hebbe' ('because I have sat (been) in the town's custody and prison').[57] In these cases, offenders had not necessarily been imprisoned as a punishment, but rather to protect the town community from them. It is worthwhile to look at these cases in a bit more detail, as they provide us with more information on the values held by the town magistrates. Analysing the *oerveden* register, it appears that many

[52] Dean, *Crime in Medieval Europe*, 121–2.
[53] DV, f. 22r (1456). Concerning Jelle, see also Chap. 4.
[54] DV, f. 119v (14 December 1471).
[55] DV, f. 37b and Reg, p. 6 (1460).
[56] LC, f. 196v (1453).
[57] Reg, on inside of binding.

who were made to swear an oath were individuals from outside of town. These individuals had most likely been unable to find anyone who would stand surety for them. As opposed to Kampen's own inhabitants, who tended to be fined for various offences and who would mostly have been able to find someone to stand surety, outsiders were imprisoned and subsequently banished after having sworn an *oervede* that they would offer no further threat to the town and its citizens. These individuals were mostly cast out without any options to return.

Individuals were also held in custody when awaiting trial. An interesting case is that of Bertolt van Hueclem who wounded a town official in office. He was sentenced to losing his hand, but the good women of the town put in a supportive word, and he was granted mercy in the shape of a 200 lb. fine. In addition, his written *oervede* had to be sealed by his father and his brother, and he would continue to be held in custody until the first of the eight terms of his fine was paid. The other seven terms would have to be paid annually following his release.[58] So, Bertolt was already in prison awaiting his trial and not only had to swear an *oervede* to be released, but two of his relatives had to seal it with him and he had to pay the first term of his fine before he was released. As such, in this case, the imprisonment also functioned as a coercive measure. Taken together, the court wanted to ensure that, although the offender was granted mercy, the seriousness of the offence was still made abundantly clear. On the other hand, there is no suggestion that Bertolt was also made to apologise to the wounded official or the magistrates, a measure that was normally laid down for offences against public officers. Perhaps the swearing of the *oervede* was considered to have been a sufficiently public gesture.

Concerning prison personnel, there are some snippets of information. In the seventeenth century, two 'stokmeesters' supervised the running of the prisons. These were two councillors who were also expected to oversee the torture of suspects.[59] In the fifteenth century, the town had a single 'stokmeester' on its payroll.[60] According to the town accounts from the late fifteenth century, Berent *de stokmeester* was paid 15 *hern* lb. (60 *stat* lb.) annually in two instalments, as well as a 6 *hern* lb. allowance for

[58] DV, f. 18r/v (1455); Reg, p. 4.

[59] Van Vliet, 'Kamper scherprechters', 89.

[60] OA, no. 402, ff. 167r (1489), 179v (1490), 191v (1491), 204v (1492), 218v (1493), 233v (1494).

clothing, presumably a livery.[61] More information about this office can be found in the *Liber Diversorum C*, a register including employment agreements of various town officials. In 1432 Huge Symonsz was hired to keep the town prisoners and to help arrest them. He would also be given wood and iron, presumably to maintain the prisons. He was paid per prisoner, and received an annual income (in 1432 this was 19½ pounds) as well as an annual allowance of fabric for clothes. He was also provided with a place to live, later specified to be at the Hagen gate. For the purposes of torture, he was provided with candles and tools by the alderman.[62] In a 1484 by-law, there is mention of 'stokmeesters'—plural—who were expected to hire two men to pray at the coffin of criminals who had been executed.[63] In addition, two *stokmeesters* are mentioned at the end of a number of entries in the register of executions from 1500 onwards, suggesting they had overseen proceedings, including, in some cases, torture.[64] It may be that there existed a situation in which two councillors were in charge of overseeing the prisons, and a third man (confusingly referred to by the same title) was appointed and paid to do the day-to-day management of the prisons. This, apparently, also included a role in the torture of suspects. Lacking other personnel, other men on the town payroll were also expected to assist with the arrest and keeping of prisoners, such as the horn blower, and the men hired to take care of the guns and the harnesses.[65]

The town had its own executioner in the fifteenth century who appears in the sources a number of times. In the seventeenth century the executioner was responsible for practising torture.[66] It may have been the same in the fifteenth century, but there is no clear evidence of this.[67] According to a by-law in the *Gulden Boeck* from the late fourteenth century, the aldermen who were involved in the torture of suspects, as well as their

[61] The term 'leverye' is only used for the executioner, but not for any of the other men on the payroll who were receiving a clothing allowance, such as watchmen and messengers, but also the glassmaker, street maker, farrier and slater (e.g. SR, ff. 179r-180r (1490)).

[62] LD, f. 170r and f. 218v.

[63] DV, f. 34v (1484).

[64] For example, Reg, p. 306 (14 July 1500), p. 287 (1520s), p. 291 (8 March 1530).

[65] LD, f. 195v (1454) and f. 196v (1453; 1457).

[66] Van Vliet, 'Kamper scherprechters', 89. See also *The Faithful Executioner* by Joel F. Harrington for a vivid picture of the career of Frantz Schmidt, executioner and torturer in sixteenth-century Nuremberg.

[67] Snijder, 'Scherprechters te Kampen', 100, does suggest that this was also the executioner's responsibility.

servants, should be recompensed with wine.[68] There is no suggestion there that the executioner was one of these servants. In fact, the next by-law concerns the payment of the executioner for conducting executions, but it does not make mention of any payments for torture. It may be that Kampen did not yet have a permanent executioner in the fourteenth century, like it did in the fifteenth. Deventer gained a permanent executioner in the second half of the fourteenth century.[69] When Johan Peecksnider was hired in Kampen in the 1440s, he was told he would have responsibility for the prisoners and for their questioning as it should be ('sal over die gevangen gaen ende verhoren als sich dat geboert'), but it is unclear how this responsibility compares to that of the 'stokmeester'.[70]

Jeroen Benders has argued that the towns in the Sticht province, which included Kampen and Deventer and which were subject to the Utrecht bishop, introduced torture after papal approval had been received in 1359. It was introduced in Deventer in 1362.[71] It is unclear how often torture took place in Kampen, as there are few direct references to it before 1500. In 1464 three men, all from out-of-town, had spent time in custody where they were 'gepinicht' (tortured) and were branded at the 'kaak' for illegal gaming activities.[72] This suggests that torture was not only used to get people to confess to the most serious crimes. Indirect evidence for torture appears in the shape of convicts taking back their confessions, which they had presumably made under pressure, when they had to confirm them in court. In 1455 Johan Jansz, a shoemaker from Deventer, had confessed to stealing a purse with money, in addition to some thefts in other towns. He was sentenced to having his ear cut off, as well as wearing a noose around his neck as a symbol of the hanging from which he had been granted mercy (see Fig. 3.5), and being banished. But when he appeared in court, he took back his confession and said he was not a thief. So, he was returned to prison.[73] Three and a half weeks later he was back in court and was

[68] GB, f. 52v (1389?).

[69] Benders, *Bestuursstructuur*, 70, n. 187.

[70] LD, f. 188v. The executioner also had other responsibilities, such as announcing the weekly street cleaning and fining inhabitants for failing to heed these calls, catching dogs and pigs and handing out fines for speeding. At the same time, he was subject to some restrictions: he was not, for example, allowed to frequent certain spaces or leave his house after 8 pm. LD, ff. 188v, 189r, 226r. Snijder, 'Scherprechters te Kampen', 101–3.

[71] Bender, *Bestuursstructuur*, 67.

[72] Reg, p. 7 (1464).

[73] DV, f. 18v (15 July 1455).

**Fig. 3.5** Johan Jansz wearing the noose (DV, 18v (15 July 1455)). (© Stadsarchief Kampen, Nederland/© City Archives Kampen, the Netherlands)

sentenced to mutilation again (see the image graphically illustrating this in Fig. 2.1) after having confessed to the theft of the purse, but apparently not to the other small thefts.[74] The evidence in this case points very clearly to the use (or at least threat) of torture. In 1484, Lambert Henricksz confessed to a small number of thefts, but he became ill 'in den stocke' and died. It may well be that his 'illness' was also the result of torture.[75]

There are more direct references in the records after 1500, most likely because of a change of clerks rather than a change in legal practices. There are a number of direct references to the use (or non-use) of torture. The most remarkable is that of a lady accused of witchcraft in 1515, who was imprisoned together with her accuser and tortured. When she did not confess, she was released. She subsequently died of her injuries in her own bed, after having received the last sacrament. Her accuser was executed for

[74] DV, f. 19r (8 August 1455).
[75] Reg, p. 230 (1484).

her false accusation two and a half months later.[76] This case tells us that torture was used on both men and women, and that an accusation was enough to justify its use. But it also suggests that the victims of torture were not always convicted. The latter is confirmed by another case from the sixteenth century in which a man was released after torture.[77] Finally, torture could also be used to get people to point to accomplices with physical descriptions of their appearance.[78]

In conclusion, a number of characteristics of penal practices in late medieval Kampen should be stressed. The magistrates had a great variation of measures at their disposal. The lower court was in charge of meting out fines for a wide range of offences, from dumping manure to the drawing of blood. The higher court of alderman and councillors dealt with the more complicated matters which required more flexibility in sentencing, such as crimes against morality. This court meted out many warnings, but also banishments, symbolic punishments, the taking away of rights and capital punishments. Less common were shameful and corporal punishments and imprisonments. Through their penal practices, the magistrates were able to communicate certain messages to the wider population. These messages could vary from warnings about behaviour which was considered to be unacceptable to well-known members of the town community, to shameful punishments and banishments to those who continued to display disruptive behaviour despite repeated warnings, to corporal and capital punishments for outsiders and a few insiders who had committed the most serious offences like theft and robbery with murder. These punishments conveyed messages of forgiveness and mercy and second (or third) chances, mainly to citizens of Kampen, but also of humiliation, shame and exclusion, especially to those crossing particular moral boundaries. Pain and terror awaited outsiders, thieves and murderers. Taken together, they displayed the magistrates' power and advertised a commitment to protecting the common weal and maintaining public order.[79]

[76] Reg, p. 272 (1515).

[77] Reg, p. 291 (18 March 1530).

[78] Vanhemelrijck, *Misdadigers tussen Recht en Beul*, 29; Zaremska, *Les bannis au Moyen Âge*, 190–4. Confessions with descriptions of accomplices' appearances can also be found in the Kampen registers after 1500, for example, Reg. p. 281 (1520).

[79] On the messages relayed through penal practices, see also Carrell, 'The ideology of punishment', 304–5, 307.

CHAPTER 4

# Exile: Banishment as a Punitive and Coercive Measure

**Abstract** The first of two main chapters, this analyses the exclusion of offenders and what this can tell us about the values of late medieval Kampen society concerning morally acceptable behaviour. This chapter firstly focuses on typologies and quantitative aspects of banishment, such as the number of exiles of various categories. It then discusses the question whether the punishment was mainly used as a punitive or coercive measure, before moving onto the distance and duration of banishments. An important part of this chapter is the discussion of aspects of gender and morality, and of social status, as this provides insights into the values of the town community. Symbolism and ceremony are discussed to establish their role in the application of authority by the magistrates. The final section analyses whether an army of exiles existed beyond Kampen's walls.

**Keywords** Crime • Morality • Gender • Social status • Ritual

It is clear that the Kampen magistrates utilised different punishments and related measures in the later middle ages to administer justice over its inhabitants and over visitors, and to communicate a range of messages about the maintenance of law and order. Within this context of punishment, banishment was reasonably common. In this chapter, various aspects of banishment in Kampen will be discussed to gain a clearer picture of the


E. Frankot, *Banishment in the Late Medieval Eastern Netherlands*,
https://doi.org/10.1007/978-3-030-88867-1_4

types of banishments, how often people were banished and for what crimes, and whether and how gender and social class played a role in the punishment. In addition, this chapter discusses whether banishment was used mainly as a punitive or a coercive measure, and to what extent ritual and ceremony played a role in banishment practices. Finally, it analyses whether the use of banishment resulted in an army of exiles outside of Kampen's walls.

## Typology, Numbers and Crimes

Authors analysing banishment have differentiated between various functions and types of banishment. Carl Hoffmann, for example, has suggested six different functions, though he states that it is not always possible to differentiate between them: banishment as (part of a) primary punishment; as a coercive measure; as a policing measure to remove unwanted people and groups; as a punishment on the basis of suspicions; as a result of not appearing in court; and as a merciful replacement for capital punishment.[1] Some of these functions are also recognisable in Kampen, though it is often difficult to differentiate between banishment as a coercive measure and as a result of not appearing in court. This is because the sequence of events is not always clear from the evidence and because the functions might overlap. There is no specific mention in Kampen of banishment being used as a merciful replacement for capital punishment, but banishments were imposed for small thefts when theft could also be punished by death.

Hoffmann also lists six different types of banishment: banishment without further specification; temporary banishment; life-long banishment; banishment with corporal punishment; banishment as a coercive measure; banishment with a fine.[2] Apart from the final type, these are also all recognisable in Kampen. In addition, it is possible to differentiate between different distances that exiles had to keep from town. However, such distances were always combined with one of the already mentioned types and it is not always possible to recognise a systematic application of different distances.[3] Distances and duration will be discussed further below. First, the focus will be on the number of banishments as primary punishments and those imposed as a coercive measure and/or a result of flight.

[1] Hoffmann, 'Der Stadtverweis', 198.
[2] Ibid., 202.
[3] See also ibid., 204.

**Table 4.1** Number of people banished according to the main registers

| *Register* | *Period* | *Total exiles* | *Male* | *Female* |
|---|---|---|---|---|
| Banishment reg. | 1447–1500 | 1267 (+18)[a] | 1180 (+15) | 87 (+3) |
| *Oerveden* reg. | 1447–1500 | 108 | 83 | 25 |
| *Digestum Vetus+Liber Causarum* | 1454–1500 | 53 (16 + 37) | 20 (10 + 10) | 33 (6 + 27) |
| Total | | 1428 (+18) | 1279 (+15) | 149 (+3) |

[a]For the 18 between brackets, see note 4

The first question to address with regard to numbers is how many people were cast out of Kampen each year and how many of these were exiled as the main punishment. Between 1447 and 1500, 1446 people were recorded in the banishment and *oerveden* registers, the *Digestum Vetus* and the *Liber Causarum* as having been banished (see Table 4.1). There is a small number of cases which appears in more than one register, but this number is negligible. Many of those banished for failure to pay their fine can be found in the lists of fines recorded in the *Liber Testium* (only covering the years 1483–93). There, on occasion, the note 'uutgt' (short for 'uutgelecht': banished) was added to indicate that someone had been exiled after the penalty had been meted out. Most of these latter entries were subsequently copied (the majority in an expanded version) into the register of banishments. As such, these do not appear separately in the table.[4] On average 26–27 people were exiled annually according to the records, keeping in mind that only the banishment and oath registers cover the first seven years of this period. There are few comparable numbers available from elsewhere in Europe. In fourteenth-century Valenciennes, with a population estimated to have been anywhere between 7500 and 30,000 inhabitants, about 53 people were banished per annum.[5] In the late twelfth and thirteenth centuries, 3–3.5 people were ousted annually from Saint-Quentin, a town which at that time was likely not much smaller than Kampen in the fifteenth century.[6] These numbers vary

[4]Eighteen people in the *Liber Testium* cannot be linked with certainty to exiles in the banishment register—a few of the offenders may be listed under an alias. For example, Lysbeth Maes, who is named with Henric Kaye (LT, f. 76v (1486)), may be the same as Betthe Bleeckster, named with Wessel Kaye in the same year (Reg, p. 134 (1486)), a *bleeckster* being a woman who bleaches cloth.

[5]Huart, 'Maintenir la paix', 12.

[6]Hamel, 'Bannis et bannissement', 130.

significantly, but without clear estimates of population numbers, it is difficult to make any useful comparisons.

Of the Kampen exiles, only a minority was sentenced to banishment in the first instance. The rest was charged with fineable offences, but they either fled the town before being caught and were sentenced to banishment in absentia (stating the fine as the primary punishment), or they were unable to pay the fine and as a result were declared banished from the town community. These two groups were recorded in the banishment register and together make up 88.7 per cent of the total. There are also at least 12 individuals in the *oerveden* register who were banished for the non-payment of fines, in addition to 15 who arranged to pay their fine following their *oervede* oath. The latter were allowed to remain in Kampen. It may be the case that offenders were taken into custody when they were caught following fineable offences, especially if they could not find people to stand surety for them. They then had to swear an *oervede* oath on their release, before they either paid their fine (or arranged for payment in instalments) or were banished for not paying it. The twelve individuals who were banished following the non-payment of their fine were partly evicted outright, whereas others were offered a possibility to return if they paid their fine. For example, Geert Hugensz, a fish merchant from Utrecht, had wounded a clerk and could not pay, so he was told not to return to Kampen ('sal niet weder in Campen komen').[7] Herman van Oldensiel was flogged and then banished for wounding the lady Stakenberg at night. The fine of 200 lb. is named, but he was told to stay at a distance of one mile from the town.[8] Arnt Geertsz too was flogged, before being banished at a distance of two miles until he could pay his fines adding up to 220 lb. (100 + 80 + 40 lb.).[9] The variation in the sentencing in these three cases suggests that the magistrates differentiated between offenders and that banishment did not always function as a coercive measure following an unpaid fine. In some cases, banishment rather became a replacement for the fine. As a result of lacking additional information, it is difficult to say whether the difference in treatment was based on the social status of the culprit (e.g. whether they were an inhabitant or not) or on the status of the victim. The question of punishment or coercion will be discussed further below.

[7] Reg, p. 23 (1491).
[8] Reg, p. 8 (1466).
[9] Reg, p. 8 (1464).

When analysing the overall numbers recorded in the same four registers, then, banishment as the primary punishment is not as common as the banishment register might at first glance suggest. Less than one in eight exiles (about three per annum) were cast out of the town as a punishment for a crime committed which was punishable by banishment. The remainder had originally been fined or they had fled from justice. That banishment after failing to pay a fine was not as prevalent everywhere is shown by the example of fourteenth-century Valenciennes, where only a small percentage (less than 4 per cent) was cast out for this reason.[10] Numbers for other towns in the Netherlands are lacking.

In Kampen, the relevant fines had mostly been meted out for violent offences. Between 1475 and 1500, for example, 501 crimes were recorded in the banishment register. In 194 more cases just a fine was recorded, but not the associated crime. Of the 501 crimes that were recorded, 285 had consisted of a wounding and another 130 were for other violent offences, such as stabbing, beating, kicking, biting and fighting. The fines for these ranged from 20 to 100 lb. (and double that if committed at night).[11] There were also 12 cases of manslaughter. Manslaughter was actually punishable by banishment, at least until a reconciliation took place.[12] In 1426 a fine for manslaughter was set at 400 lb. and such a fine is recorded on occasion.[13] It is likely that in most cases offenders would have fled the scene of the crime after a killing so they could arrange a reconciliation through mediation by others from a safe distance. Altogether 427 out of 501 known crimes in the banishment register between 1475 and 1500 were violent (85.2 per cent).

There would have been few people in Kampen who would have been able to easily pay the large fines set for violent crimes. For example, the highest paid official on the council's payroll, the town's senior secretary, was paid 260 lb. annually.[14] The guards were paid between 60 and 112 lb. per annum. The average amount that debtors were paying back in instalments per year (see Chap. 5) was between 30 and 44 lb. Considering rentals of town properties, the largest amount was due for the bridge, namely

[10] In total 97 out of 2600 were banished for unpaid fines. Huart, 'Maintenir la paix', 11.

[11] Originally the punishment for a wounding at night was the loss of a hand (GB, f. 39r (1334)), but in practice a fine of 200 lb. was meted out.

[12] BvR, f. 22v (1385).

[13] GB, f. 48r (1426). For example, Reg, p. 140 (1490).

[14] In the original source, these payments are stated in *hern* lb.: 65 *hern* lb. for the senior secretary, between 12½ and 28 *hern* lb. for the guards. On currency, see Chap. 3, n. 5.

2000 lb. in 1490, which was paid in ten instalments. Most other rents were below 400 lb., and most were paid in a number of terms and often with the help of others.[15] It can be assumed that these rentals were only taken up by the more affluent of Kampen's citizens, but even they rarely paid more than 120 lb. at a time for them. As such, only the elite would most likely have been able to pay a high fine immediately.[16] Possibly the magistrates had taken the likelihood that many violent offenders would flee the town or would be unable to pay a fine (and as a result be banished) into account when they set their fines, perhaps considering this as a relatively straightforward way of ridding the town of undesirables. I will return to this below.

Of course, we should ask ourselves whether violent behaviour in itself was considered to be undesirable in late medieval society. It is well-established that (violent) conflict was common at this time.[17] In addition, confrontations have been shown to have developed according to a set sequence of acts, from verbal exchanges to potentially drawing blood and killing an opponent. Such 'rituals of confrontation' have been recognised in different geographical contexts, such as England, France, Germany and Italy.[18] The confrontations often followed a set formula, starting with verbal abuse, followed by gestures and eventually leading to blows. At any stage in these confrontations opponents could retreat, either of their own volition or because they had been convinced by bystanders. In the final stages, this violence could lead to injury or even death, but it has been argued that, because of their ritualised nature, most confrontations ended without any bloodshed. Charles Pythian-Adams, for example, has shown that striking with the flat of the sword, rather than the edge, was common.[19] Similarly, Trevor Dean has pointed to the use of sword blades.[20] As such, the intention was to bruise or hurt an opponent, but not to draw blood, maim or kill. A wide variety of 'weapons' could potentially be used:

[15] SR, ff. 172v-175v.

[16] Concerning high fines and the inability of offenders to pay them, see also Næss and Österberg, 'Sanctions, agreements, sufferings', 147.

[17] See, for example, Zaremska, *Les bannis au Moyen Âge*, 152; Hoffmann, 'Der Stadtverweis', 214.

[18] Pythian-Adams, 'Rituals of personal confrontation'; Gauvard, *'De grace especial'*, 707–45; Schuster, *Stadt vor Gericht*, 86–90; Dean, *Crime and Justice in Late Medieval Italy*, Ch. 9.

[19] Pythian-Adams, 'Rituals of personal confrontation', 83.

[20] Dean, *Crime and Justice in Late Medieval Italy*, 169.

jugs were common in Kampen, but anything that came to hand could be used to cast a blow.[21] This suggests that many confrontations were not pre-meditated (Peter Arnade and Walter Prevenier call them 'unplanned'),[22] but occurred in social situations, such as in various drinking establishments. The use of any kind of weapon incurred the same fine in Kampen: for example, the pouring of milk at someone ('om dat sie na lange Johan gegoten heft mit melke')[23] resulted in the same 40 lb. fine as stabbing at someone with a knife without wounding them. At the same time a blow with a fist incurred a fine of 2 or 10 lb. It may be that pouring milk as a gesture in an escalating confrontation had the same symbolic meaning as pulling out a knife. In both cases an item was thrust towards someone to make a certain statement. The item could potentially be used to cause more damage, both physically and to one's reputation, though it is questionable that pouring milk would cause any physical damage.

It has been argued that most confrontations did not go beyond verbal abuse or the use of fists, and indeed, in Kampen in 1490, 27 people incurred a fine for using offensive language and 17 had used their fists.[24] However, there were also 16 individuals charged with wounding someone and 1 with manslaughter. Virtually all of these individuals ended up being banished for failing to pay their fine. It appears, then, that, if ritualistic confrontations were also part of legal culture in Kampen (which they may well have been judging by the strict categorisation of violence as reflected in fines), these did not prevent a relatively high proportion of woundings. They also did not avert a higher number of deaths than, for example, in Konstanz which had a similar population size. In Cracow in the late fourteenth century, the number of deaths was much higher again.[25] This variation suggests that we need to be careful issuing universal truths about ritualistic violence and the prevention of serious injury in late medieval Europe.

[21] See also ibid.; Schuster, *Stadt vor Gericht*, 90.

[22] Concerning unplanned violence and differences between young men and heads of households, see Arnade and Prevenier, *Honor, Vengeance, and Social Trouble*, 82–9.

[23] Reg, p. 84 (1451).

[24] See, for example, Schuster, *Stadt vor Gericht*, 87; Dean, *Crime and Justice in Late Medieval Italy*, 169.

[25] In Konstanz, there were 9 deaths between 1430 and 1460, when there were 16 between 1480 and 1499 in Kampen. In Cracow, there were at least 62 in 1380–84, on a population of 10,000. Schuster, *Stadt vor Gericht*, 89; Zaremska, *Les bannis au Moyen Âge*, 152.

The setting of high fines for various acts of violence may also be considered in the context of the rituals of confrontation which sought to prevent the escalation of violence. Every step in the confrontation was fined differently, and fines were not deviated from. The occurrence of a wounding meant that a conflict had moved far beyond its initial stages in which opponents were offered de-escalation opportunities on a number of occasions, potentially with the help of bystanders. Individuals who let conflicts get out of hand received high fines without recourse to a flexible application of these, or alternative punishments. No specific circumstances were taken into account, apart from the aggravating ones in which an act was committed. As such, there was a clear link between the offence and the punishment, and it was obvious that every offender was expected to take direct responsibility for their act. At the same time, when a fine was paid immediately, the offence had no further repercussions.[26]

Violence was not an offence that constituted an obstacle to life in the community.[27] The judgement of immoral behaviour was quite different in this respect. In such cases, the magistrates were much more flexible in their punishment. This was perhaps because such behaviour could be considered an obstacle to life in the community, at least from the perspective of the culprits' neighbours who denounced them. At the same time, the failure to take responsibility for violent acts (which could, of course, simply be an inability to pay a high fine) also resulted in an exclusion from the community. However, it was not normally the violent act that was the problem, but rather the failure to pay. The link between morality and debt will be discussed further in Chap. 5.

As a punishment, banishment was common especially in cases of sexual misconduct or other behaviour considered to have been immoral as recorded in the *Digestum Vetus* and the *Liber Causarum*. These were cases that were generally decided before the full council and were thus apparently considered to require the full strength of 24 magistrates, as opposed to the fineable offences which were dealt with by the two burgomasters. The majority of banishment punishments (about two-thirds) were, however, recorded in the *oerveden* register. In these, it is not often detailed what the offenders were punished for. Most of those that do were for small

[26] There are a few exceptions in which individuals were banished for violent acts which led to potential maiming, such as Lubbert of Amersfoort who had hurt his victim's eye. Reg, p. 127 (1478).

[27] Concerning this, see Zaremska, *Les bannis au Moyen Âge*, 73.

thefts (nine offenders), vagabondage (five men in a single case) and adultery (four people). Taking the cases from these registers together, banishment as a punishment was most regularly imposed for crimes against morality, followed by petty theft. This may have set in motion (or continued) a push towards a life on the road robbing and stealing. Such a life might ultimately lead to the gallows. Whether the casting out of vagabonds was a usual occurrence is not clear, as the five men who were banished for vagabondage were all evicted at the same time.

Banishment for petty theft was not uncommon in late medieval and early modern Europe. It has also been recorded in medieval Ghent, Saint-Quentin and Poland, and in early modern Turku, Scotland and Augsburg.[28] In addition, it became more common for people to be banished for vagabondage, potentially combined with transient theft, in the early modern period, such as in Turku, Augsburg and Ulm.[29] Kampen was also not alone in banishing sexual offenders. This was, for example, evident in Turku for outsiders (insiders were fined or received penance), in medieval Poland, and in early modern Scotland, Augsburg and Ulm (especially of citizens).[30] In some places, individuals were banished outright for violent behaviour, such as in medieval Poland and Saint-Quentin, and in early modern Ulm.[31] In Ghent, banishments were used as reduced punishments for very young or very old culprits.[32] Banishments were also used as coercive measures in different places in Europe, such as medieval Deventer, Saint-Quentin and early modern Augsburg.[33] In medieval Cracow, banishment was also used to force a culprit to start negotiations after a manslaughter.[34] In other places, individuals were sometimes required to pay a sum of money in

[28] Van Eetveld, 'Vrouwencriminaliteit', 32; Hamel, 'Bannis et bannissement', 130; Zaremska, *Les bannis au Moyen Âge*, 132; Laitinen, 'Banishment', 552–3; Ewan, 'Crossing borders and boundaries', 240; Tyler, 'Refugees and reform', 92.

[29] Laitinen, 'Banishment', 552–3; Tyler, 'Refugees and reform', 87; Coy, *Strangers and Misfits*, 30.

[30] Laitinen, 'Banishment', 555; Zaremska, *Les bannis au Moyen Âge*, 132; Ewan, 'Crossing borders and boundaries', 240; Tyler, 'Refugees and reform', 87; Coy, *Strangers and Misfits*, 29, 81.

[31] Zaremska, *Les bannis au Moyen Âge*, 131, and Jeziorski, 'Die Strafe der Ausweisung', 37; Hamel, 'Bannis et bannissement', 130; Coy, *Strangers and Misfits*, 29.

[32] Van Eetveld, 'Vrouwencriminaliteit', 32.

[33] Benders, *Bestuursstructuur*, 175; Hamel, 'Bannis et bannissement', 124–5; Hoffmann, 'Der Stadtverweis', 224.

[34] Zaremska, *Les bannis au Moyen Âge*, 130.

order to return after an exile, such as in medieval Fritzlar and Ghent.[35] Throughout Europe, banishments were mostly imposed in cases of petty theft, vagabondage and sexual offences. In addition, perpetrators of violent crimes regularly ended up ousted from communities, either directly, or as a result of flight or the non-payment of the associated fine. As such, individuals were banished for a wide range of crimes. As others have also concluded, banishment was a very flexible punishment and measure which could be used for different purposes and in various different guises, and which was cheap to execute. It was also easily reversible and, especially when it was not combined with ritualistic displays, did not permanently damage a culprit's reputation.[36]

Sometimes, banishments in Kampen were imposed together with other punishments. These cases are found in the *oerveden* register. It seems that a group of men and women were caught following their fineable or other offences and put in custody. They were subsequently made to swear an oath before they were subjected to a punishment such as banishment or a flogging and banishment. The possibility to be subjected to a flogging in addition to banishment was a likely incentive for people guilty of fineable offences to flee. Of course, there were plenty of others who were not imprisoned before paying their fine, probably because they found people to vouch for them, but the threat of imprisonment and flogging was likely enough of an incentive for someone to choose to flee the town and negotiate the payment of a fine from elsewhere.

There were also a few individuals charged with adultery who were kept in custody and then were punished in accordance with the by-laws by being subjected to the 'kaak' and paying an 80 lb. fine. In 1469, for example, Johan Claesz the fuller and Bettken a wool comber swore an oath after having been found in adultery and spending time in custody. They were put on the 'kaak' and were subsequently banished for their 80 lb. fines. Johan had to stay at a distance of ten miles on pain of losing his hand, while Bettken was only banished from the town freedom until she could pay.[37] Neither seems to have returned to Kampen, as the entry remains undeleted. A similar case is that against Thijs, the son of Jacob

[35] Von Brockdorf, 'Die Strafe des Stadtverweises', 49; Van Eetveld, 'Vrouwencriminaliteit', 10.

[36] Coy, *Strangers and Misfits*, 15, 111. Concerning flexibility, see also, for example, Zaremska, *Les bannis au Moyen Âge*, 74; Maurer, 'Erzwungene Ferne', 201; Von Brockdorf, 'Die Strafe des Stadtverweises', 53.

[37] Reg, p. 10 (1469).

Boymansz, and Mense, the daughter of Henric Buysks. In their case there is no specific mention of imprisonment, but seeing that the oath was taken to prevent revenge after a stint in prison, Thijs and Mense most likely were kept in custody for a time too. In this case, there is no mention of a fine either: Thijs was sentenced to a banishment at a distance of five miles (on pain of losing his hand) and Mense at a distance of one mile on pain of carrying the stone.[38] It is notable that in these cases the women were allowed to stay closer to the town. This could be construed as having been a slightly lighter punishment, but it may also indicate that the magistrates appreciated that a banishment was riskier for a lone woman than it was for a lone man. As we will see below, men were not normally punished more harshly for sexual crimes.

Other offences that could be punished with banishment according to the *oerveden* register were meddling in counterfeit goods, defamation and begging using false documents. In the latter case, the culprit had spoken 'dishonourable words of defamation' ('oneerlike woirde van diffamacie') about monasteries and clerics, obviously more serious insults than those usually fined with 2 or 10 lb. It might well be that the woman who had spoken these words, Henric de Kemmester (a wool comber?), already had a bad reputation and few respectable people that could or were willing to vouch for her, as she was made to keep a distance of at least five miles without any reprieve.[39]

There are a few other cases of individuals, likely of marginal status for whatever reason, who were punished differently by the Kampen magistrates. In 1455 a man known as the 'limping man' ('dat hinkende manneken') was punished for a number of offences. It was known that he had killed a man in Emmerich before. He was now flogged for wounding a man in his hand, throwing a stone at another man's chest and hurling rocks at a glass window. A vivid image of a man seemingly only wearing a garment covering his nether regions tied to the pillory and flogged by the executioner with a birch rod accompanies the entry. The man's back is marked by the beating (see Fig. 3.3).[40] But apparently the flogging did not have the desired effect ('mer hee was doef daer um') and he was banned from the town. So, in this case, the court did not go the usual route of fining, nor does the case appear to have been dealt with by the burgomasters, as was

[38] Reg, p. 15 (1479).
[39] Reg, p. 20 (1487).
[40] DV, f. 16v.

the norm for fineable offences. Instead, the man, who was marginalised even by the simple act of only referring to him as 'the limping man', was flogged, and only when that did not help, finally banished. It seems, then, that the council wanted to make an example of this man by flogging him publicly and perhaps literally beating him into submission. But it seems that this public ritual did not go according to plan, perhaps because the man only became less submissive as the beating went on. Gerd Schwerhoff has already pointed to the risks of public shaming in that a delinquent might use the podium for their own devices, and spectators could potentially turn on the magistrates.[41] In this case, it appears that the magistrates managed to regain control of the situation when, as the final act, the man was cast out, likely accompanied by the same magistrates, the executioner, crowds and lots of noise.

Others were marginalised by their names too. In 1457 a woman referred to as 'raging Jutte' ('rasende Jutte') appeared before the council. It was reported that she had already received a warning in 1453 for adulterous behaviour, but that she was found in adultery again by the councillors themselves who she apparently showed her behind in an act of defiance ('liet onse raetsvrende in den stert sien'). In addition, her neighbours complained to the council about adultery, procuring and similar things. She was put in custody awaiting a punishment on the 'kaak' or carrying the stone, in accordance with the warning that she had received in 1453. But on the next court day, the councillors had changed their minds and banished her instead.[42] In this case, we do actually know Jutte's full name. She appears on an undated list of couples who were probably thought to be adulterous as Jutte van Ors op den Bilt, together with a man called Ludeken. A note was added to their names saying 'Dat is rasende Jutte'.[43]

A final case that should be mentioned in this context is from the same period as the previous two, but in this case the individual was not banished. In 1456 it was unanimously decided that Jelle, whose portrait accompanies the text, should be put in the 'Wulentoerne'. Jelle, whose name suggests a Friesian heritage, had inflicted a punch on a man known as the duke of the Orient in a tavern, so that the victim had lost two teeth and gained a very ugly face ('een alteleliken aensichte').[44] Again, normally such an offence should have been dealt with by the lower court and have

[41] Schwerhoff, 'Verordnete Schande?', 173.

[42] DV, f. 27r (28 June 1457).

[43] DV, f. 21ar-v.

[44] DV, f. 22r (January 1456).

resulted in a fine. In this case, though, Jelle was not flogged or banished, but he was locked up in a tower. It seems that Jelle was a character that the magistrates did not want to cast out of their community completely, perhaps because of a mental disability. If that was indeed the case, and perhaps depending on the severity of this disability, Jelle may have been locked up indefinitely in this tower, which is not mentioned anywhere else. He does not reappear elsewhere in the sources.

So occasionally the council deviated from the usual course of action in their punishment practices, apparently when it concerned particular marginal individuals. In addition, the magistrates on occasion appeared to marginalise people through their naming practices. Today we are used to courts and official institutions only utilising our full names, but in the later middle ages there were, of course, no standard naming practices. Nonetheless, the use of nicknames like 'rasende Jutte', adding a pejorative adjective to someone's name, suggests a bias that can only have influenced decisions negatively.[45] At the same time, we see that Jutte was not punished on her first conviction; she received a warning and was only actually punished four years later when her continued immoral behaviour was a source of concern to both council and neighbours. This is a topic that I will return to below when discussing social status.

## Punishment Versus Coercive Measure

The cases of outright banishment can be characterised relatively straightforwardly as punishments. The offenders had violated the town and town community's formal and informal rules and were punished by being excluded, either temporarily, permanently or until further notice, from this community. The use of additional punishments, which were mainly corporal and/or shameful, served to further stress and make public this exclusion. Mutilation marked offenders for life, making it difficult not only to re-enter Kampen society, but to join any community.

The other banishments are more difficult to characterise, also because it is impossible to recognise the sequence of events in many of the cases. Did offenders flee immediately after their offence, did they leave when they were charged or were they banished after their conviction when they

[45] Arnade and Prevenier, *Honor, Vengeance, and Social Trouble*, 181, noted that certain labels attached to people, such as prostitute, actress, wife or harlot, fixed their identities and assigned to them certain 'motives, justification and culpability'.

were unable to pay their fine? In some cases, it is likely to have been the latter option, as in these cases their fine might have been listed among other fines initially, with the note 'uutg' added later. The same is the case for some of the entries recorded in the *oerveden* register. For the offenders not listed in either of these sources, it is likely to be one of the other two options. The question is whether we should consider the banishment in these cases as a coercive measure or as a punishment.

Richard Ireland and Guy Geltner have argued that imprisonment for debt should not be considered as a purely coercive measure. Debt, be it private or public (including fines), was 'viewed as a form of sin or social offence which merited punishment'.[46] As such, debtors were not imprisoned solely to coerce them into paying, but also to punish them for their breach of faith. In addition, as Geltner argues, the premise of coercion is that the object is reluctant to do something. But poorer inmates were often incapable of ever paying off their debt or fine rather than being reluctant but, nonetheless, were imprisoned for life.[47] The same can be said for banishment, although there is a marked difference between being held in one place until a debt was paid, or being wholly excluded from a space. In both cases, an offender could no longer conduct their activities in the same fashion as before. As a convict, however, they were not excluded from their community entirely, but rather contained. As Geltner states, they were marginalised, but not liminalised. In this way, urban magistrates could maintain social order without excluding a convict completely.[48]

For an exile, the exclusion was more or less complete, though perhaps temporary, but there were also options to start afresh in a different place. Exiles were also more mobile. This mobility can make us question the efficacy of using banishment as a coercive measure and, as such, whether the magistrates used it as such, or at least whether they used it as such for everyone. As was suggested by the evidence from the *oerveden* register, not everyone was offered the possibility to redeem themselves. Of course, for those who had built up a life in Kampen and had strong ties to the town and the community, a banishment may have been effective in

[46] Ireland, 'Theory and Practice', 57.

[47] Ibid.; Geltner, *The Medieval Prison*, 52–3, 101.

[48] Geltner, *The Medieval Prison*, 4, 106–8, referring to this practice as 'rough tolerance'. For the conceptual relationship between banishment and imprisonment, see also Van Caenegem, *Geschiedenis van het strafrecht*, 228.

coercing them to pay (or to arrange for a payment in terms). It is different for those who did not have such strong ties. These men and women might have decided to build up a life elsewhere and it is likely that the town magistrates were not sorry to see them go if this was the case. Banishment then became a method to get rid of the undeserving poor. Poverty in itself was not a reason to exclude defaulters permanently. As will become clear in Chap. 5, the magistrates were flexible in arranging terms. A final consideration concerning coercion is that one can wonder to what extent one can coerce someone who no longer resides in one's jurisdiction.

The banishment for failure to pay a fine was therefore probably largely punitive. Of course, the non-payment of fines did not constitute a breach of faith in the same way that the non-payment of a debt did. But being part of the town community meant an agreement to abide by its formal and informal rules and to take responsibility when breaking them. As such, a failure to pay a fine and, ergo, to face up to one's responsibilities could be considered a breach of faith. Of course, such responsibilities were much easier to keep when one's finances were stable, and one had an extensive network.

It could be argued that the failure to pay a fine meant that an offender could not be punished in accordance with the by-laws. Banishment could then be considered an alternative punishment for the original offence. But in many cases, offenders were still expected to pay the full fine in order to be allowed to return. So, rather than being an alternative punishment for the original offence, it figured as a punitive measure for the failure to pay. This is also how it is portrayed in the town's by-laws, according to which a flogging needed to precede the lawbreaker's banishment (although this flogging appears to be largely absent from legal practice in the second half of the fifteenth century). However, in some cases banishment for unpaid fines may actually have acted and/or have been meant as an alternative punishment. When culprits in the *oerveden* register were told not to return after failing to pay a fine, the banishment was likely to have been considered as an alternative punishment.

Comparing the situations of debtors in Kampen and Italy, the former were better off as soon as they had arranged for repayment as they then became full members of urban society once again. This is opposed to most Italian debtors who remained in prison until their debt was paid off completely or a certain time had passed.[49] In Deventer, too, debts appear to

[49] Geltner, *The Medieval Prison*, 58–60.

have been expected to be paid in full before an exiled person was allowed to return.[50] While banished, the Kampen exiles were most likely worse off: living a life of insecurity outside the safety of the town bounds, without their social network to protect them. Geltner has argued that, contrary to the bad press that they have generally received, medieval prisons were no 'hellholes'.[51] Prisons were situated in the medieval city and inmates had more ready access to friends and family than exiles did. Of course, prison life was still fairly unpleasant, but overall, probably less risky than being banished.

## Distance, Duration and Additional Punishments

The banishment register does not include information on the duration of exiles or the distance that the banished had to keep from the town. Presumably there was a set distance, most likely outside the area of the town freedom, or one mile beyond that, the so-called *banmijl*. This *banmijl* radius also appears to have been used in at least two other towns in the lordship of the Utrecht bishop: Utrecht and Deventer.[52] In addition, the banishment would remain valid until the fine was paid. There is no indication anywhere in the sources that a certain time away from the town could redeem any amount of fine. This does not necessarily mean that a period outside the town walls could not replace a low fine, but there is simply no information available anywhere in the sources. The possibility to replace a fine with banishment did exist elsewhere in the Netherlands: in Dordrecht every 6 months of banishment was worth 40 'Holland schellingen'. In Utrecht it was possible to choose a banishment for a restricted period instead of paying a fine for gambling.[53]

The banishments which were meted out as punishments mostly did include notes on the distance from the town and about a third also on the

[50] Benders, *Bestuursstructuur*, 177.

[51] Ibid., 80.

[52] Berents, *Misdaad in de Middeleeuwen*, 48; Benders, *Bestuursstructuur*, 177. The medieval mile in the Netherlands was much longer than the current mile. It is considered to have been the approximate distance that a person could walk within one hour, that is approx. 5 km, but the distance varied throughout the Netherlands. Cf. the different miles used in Germany and Switzerland, Marchal, 'Von der Stadt', 245. In medieval Ghent (and presumably the other Flemish towns) people were banished not from the town but from the county of Flanders as a whole. Eetveld, 'Vrouwencriminaliteit', 9.

[53] Van Herwaarden, *Opgelegde bedevaarten*, 298; Berents, *Misdaad in de Middeleeuwen*, 48.

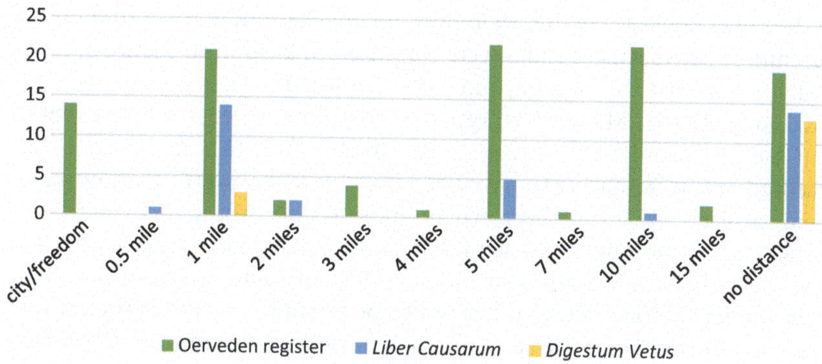


**Fig. 4.1** Distances of banishment in different registers

duration of the stay. The distance ranged from outside the town or town freedom to 15 miles (see Fig. 4.1).[54] There is a lot of variation in the distances, but the most commonly used were one mile, five miles and ten miles, in addition to a banishment from the town or town freedom. There is also a significant number of entries which does not include a distance. Distances in miles were used elsewhere in Europe too: they were common in German and Swiss towns, for example, but town magistrates there also indicated distance in different ways. In some cases, features in the landscape were named, such as rivers or mountains, and in others legal boundaries beyond the town, which were often indicated by physical markers such as stone crosses or pillars, were used. There could be great variation in the distances thus indicated, from nearby to faraway rivers and mountains, sometimes up to 150 or even 200 kilometres away. Some were banished across the Alps into Italian-speaking territories. The added advantage of physical features in the landscape was that they were easily recognisable which made it difficult for exiles to talk their way out of being found on the wrong side of them.[55] Such variation is not recorded in Kampen and it is unknown whether any physical markers were erected to indicate the 'banmijl' or other distances.

[54] Almost all of the entries in the *oerveden* register and the *Liber Causarum* include a distance, whereas only three entries in the *Digestum Vetus* contain this information. The latter two only rarely include a note on the duration.

[55] Maurer, 'Erzwungene Ferne', 202, 205–6; Marchal, 'Von der Stadt', 229, 245.

It is also unclear whether there was any mechanism in place to monitor or enforce the distances exiles were supposed to keep from Kampen, especially seeing that the area beyond the town freedom was outside its jurisdiction.[56] Helmut Maurer has argued that the longer distances were meted out to also protect the towns' hinterlands.[57] But, as Guy Marchal has pointed out, it is unlikely to have been possible to know exactly how many miles a place was from the town bounds. Rather, these miles indicated either shorter or longer distances that outcasts needed to keep from town and, as such, signified a less or more significant exclusion from the town community.[58] Nonetheless, it needed to be possible to enforce the various verdicts. Amsterdam for that reason apparently requested from Charles V that milestones be placed around the city, so that distances could be more easily enforced, and exiles would not have an excuse when they were found too close to town.[59] This suggests that policing forces were dispatched to monitor the presence of banished individuals. In cities like Bamberg, Nürnberg, Speyer and Ulm, too, soldiers were sent out on surveillance to check the roads leading from the city, as far as 50–60 kilometres away. As the neighbouring regions were generally subject to noble lords, agreements were set up for the specific purpose of capturing exiles who stayed in the area illegally.[60] It may well be that similar checks were conducted from Kampen, though there is no evidence that anyone was caught outside the town bounds in an area that was off-limits to them. The indication of distances in the sources and the monitoring of these suggest that people were expected to have some sense of geography and distances. As Marchal has stated, the sources that survive were written by those in power, but in order to be able to enforce the verdicts, they needed to have been understood by those who they concerned.[61]

The duration of stay was less straightforward than the distance. A few were banished from Kampen for five or ten years. Others were banished until further notice (occasionally it stated specifically: until messengers were sent to get them back), until the offender learned to behave themselves or until a fine was paid. So, these all correspond to Hoffmann's temporary exiles. There were also banishments without further

[56] Coy, 'Beggars at the gates', 637.
[57] Maurer, 'Erzwungene Ferne', 203.
[58] Marchal, 'Von der Stadt', 249.
[59] Maurer, 'Erzwungene Ferne', 203.
[60] Ibid., 203–4.
[61] Marchal, 'Von der Stadt', 225–6.

specification: in one or two cases there was no mention of distance or duration of stay, and in others there was only a very general statement that someone was banned ('der stad verboden', 'uutgelacht', 'niet weder comen', the last of which suggests a banishment for life). Finally, there were some who were banished permanently. These were cast out either for life or for eternity. The difference may lie in the question whether or not an exile could be buried in Kampen after their death or not, though it may be that there was only a symbolic difference between the two. This variation in duration existed elsewhere too, but there are clear differences in the general practices locally. In Cracow, in the late middle ages, for example, banishments were mostly for life on pain of capital punishment. There were some which were shorter, like six months, one year or ten years, but the majority were sentences for life.[62] In medieval Ghent, individuals were mostly sentenced to very long banishments, with an average of 50 years, but ranging from three years to eternally. However, many apparently negotiated a return against payment within two to three years.[63] In medieval Saint-Quentin, manslaughterers who fled were exiled eternally, but those convicted for moveable debts or thefts received a temporary banishment.[64] In Luzern, banishments were mostly in months, rather than years.[65] Overall, then, it is difficult to discern a shared legal culture when it comes to the duration of banishment and its relation to various crimes.

The banishments recorded in the *oerveden* register were mostly meted out after the offender had already spent some time in prison. In total 43 of 108 persons that were banished according to this register also received additional punishments, especially floggings, but also public punishments on the pillory ('kaak'), the cutting off of an ear (or part thereof) or branding.[66] Ears were always cut off as a punishment for theft, but some thieves were just flogged. The pillory was generally used for adulterers, although a counterfeiter was also displayed on the pillory wearing a paper hat, before being banished for eternity and at a distance of ten miles.[67] The

[62] Zaremska, *Les bannis au Moyen Âge*, 132.

[63] Van Eetveld, 'Vrouwencriminaliteit', 9–10.

[64] Hamel, 'Bannis et bannissement', 125.

[65] Marchal, 'Von der Stadt', 241.

[66] It is noteworthy that no banishments were recorded in the *oerveden* register after 1491. There is no sign of any abating of banishments in the other registers.

[67] Reg, p. 14 (30 September 1476). This is the only time that the punishment of wearing a paper hat is mentioned anywhere in the sources.

punishment for counterfeit goods was also meted out at the pillory: one offender's wool combs were burnt there before he himself was banished.[68]

From 1464 onwards especially (only rarely before) a majority of oath-taking exiles also received a warning not to return to Kampen during their banishment on pain of various punishments, many of them corporal or capital. This deviates from the general rule of an 80 lb. fine as discussed above. There is no clear correlation between the distance of the banishment and the seriousness of this warning, though long distances (10 or 15 miles) were only ever combined with capital punishment, or the cutting off of ear or hand. Short distances were, however, also combined with capital punishment.[69] There is no evidence that such punishments were actually executed, but that may be because none of the exiles actually returned. Similar threats or regulations existed elsewhere: in medieval Saint-Quentin harsh punishments were meted out for illegal returns.[70] In medieval Ghent, capital punishment was laid down for the breaking of eternal banishments and actually executed.[71] In medieval Valenciennes, the threat was not a corporal or capital punishment, but a permanent banishment.[72] These threats have in common their aim: trying to convince exiles not to return.

## The Role of Gender and Morality

Considering all banishments, the proportion of women who were exiled was only small: 152 out of the 1446 offenders in Table 4.1 (10.5 per cent). In the register of banishment, the numbers are even lower: 90 out of 1285 (7 per cent). This is because many more men were fined, and the highest fines were also mainly incurred by men, for various forms of violence. Nonetheless, about a third of the women in this register were also banished after failing to pay a fine dealt out for violence.[73] The proportions in the other three registers are very different. In the *oerveden* register almost a quarter (23.1 per cent) of the banished were women, in the *Digestum Vetus* more than a third (37.5 per cent), whereas in the *Liber*

[68] Reg, p. 1 (18 December 1447).

[69] Offences are mentioned too irregularly to be able to establish any correlation between crime and conditional punishment.

[70] Hamel, 'Bannis et bannissement', 130.

[71] Van Eetveld, 'Vrouwencriminaliteit', 125.

[72] Huart, 'Maintenir la paix', 14.

[73] A small majority of these cases concerned violence against other women.

*Causarum* it was almost three-quarters (73 per cent). As a primary punishment, therefore, banishment was dealt out to relatively many women; 62 out of 161 banished offenders were female (38.5 per cent).

This high percentage is due to the fact that banishments were often administered as a punishment for sexual offences, offences concerning which relatively many women were charged. Of the ten cases in the *oerveden* register in which a crime perpetrated by a woman is mentioned, five had been meted out for adultery and one for procuring (of the other four, two were for theft, one for defamation and one for violence). In the *Liber Causarum* 19 out of 27 women had been punished for adultery or facilitating prostitution (against two out of ten men).[74] Nine out of ten women (against three out of six men) in the *Digestum Vetus* had been sentenced to banishment for sexual offences, the tenth not mentioning a crime. In a number of cases of adultery only the woman was banished; the man got away with a warning.

In fact, in many cases of sexually offensive conduct, the offenders received warnings, both men and women, despite the relatively hefty punishments laid down in the by-laws. Several by-laws were recorded in the town registers in the second half of the 1450s, especially around the times that the Franciscan Observant friar Brugman visited the town in 1455 and 1458 and preached against lewd priests, immoral town councils, adulterers, drunks, gamblers and prostitutes.[75] The by-laws proscribed adultery and 'kwade herberg' ('bad inn': facilitating illegal sexual acts) on punishment of banishment or the 'kaak' and a fine of 80 lb. each.[76] Nonetheless, in 1463 two women named Swarte Gese and Asselе (see Fig. 4.2) were given a warning for 'kwade herberg' and procuring.[77] Similarly, Herman Druuchschere and his wife Hille (see Fig. 4.3) were given a warning in 1467.[78] All four offenders are portrayed by the clerk in images accompanying the entries. Apart, perhaps, from Hille, all have lowered heads,

[74] Two of the 19 were in combination with misbehaviour.

[75] DV, f. 19v (1455), f. 31r (1458). Brand and Frankot, 'Das Kampener Stadtbuch', 58–59. Between 1455 and 1463 Brugman visited a large number of towns in various parts of the Netherlands, where he preached for hours. With regard to his sojourn in Bolsward in 1455, see Robijn, *Het recht van een vrije Friese stad*, 99–103. More generally, see Lettinck, *Praten als Brugman*.

[76] DV, f. 21r (5 December 1455; three by-laws, one of which was subsequently deleted); f. 21v (18 December 1455); f. 21v (20 December 1455); f. 30v (1 July 1458).

[77] DV, f. 54r (1463).

[78] DV, f. 75v (23 May 1467).

Fig. 4.2 Swarte Gese and Assele (DV, f. 54r (1463)). (© Stadsarchief Kampen, Nederland/© City Archives Kampen, the Netherlands)

Fig. 4.3 Herman Druuchschere and Hille (DV, f. 75v (23 May 1467)). (© Stadsarchief Kampen, Nederland/© City Archives Kampen, the Netherlands)

presumably to suggest their humility before the court when receiving their warnings.

In court, sexual offenders were given warnings, as were others who misbehaved, especially those accused of domestic violence.[79] These warnings sometimes included specific punishments that would be inflicted on repeating an offence, but at other times would be vaguer, as indicated earlier. Terms such as 'the offender will be punished so that they will figure as an example (or a mirror) to others', 'the court will consider the punishment', 'the offender will be sentenced harshly' or 'the offender shall not know their punishment' were used. This suggests that the court often judged people on a case-by-case basis and took personal circumstances into account.[80] Such flexibility in judging is also in evidence elsewhere, such as in early modern Ulm, where the court took into account various personal circumstances.[81] Unfortunately, in Kampen these circumstances are not often quoted, and we are therefore mostly left in the dark as to why one person was let off easily, whereas others were punished more harshly. For example, in 1484 Johan Fedde and his wench (in Dutch the word can be used for both servant and prostitute) confessed to having committed adultery. A child was also born from this union. The council decided that the two could not remain in Kampen any longer and had to distance themselves two miles from the town jurisdiction.[82] In 1492, on the other hand, it was decided that Cornelis van den Busch, the husband of Mette Busen, and Large Gerryt, the wench, should no longer have any contact, in any sense of the word, and that Cornelis should live peacefully together with his wife like a good husband was expected to do. If they were caught again, they would be punished shamefully on the 'kaak' to set an example to others.[83] It may be that Johan Fedde's affair had been going on for longer—the evidence of a child born from their union certainly suggests this—but there may also be other reasons for the difference in treatment.

At other times it is clear why someone was sentenced to be banished: a combination of crimes of adultery and procuring usually resulted in a

[79] Cf. with the magistrates of Leiden taking women into protection against aggressive men, Blockmans and Neijzen, 'Functions of fiction', 275.

[80] This flexibility of administering the law is mainly to be found in the higher court of aldermen. The lower court appears to have adhered strictly to the fines laid down in the bylaws. See also below.

[81] Coy, *Strangers and Misfits*, 25.

[82] LC, f. 16v (3 October 1484).

[83] LC, f. 34v (19 July 1492).

banishment. In 1476, for example, the council decided that Mette van Epe was to leave the town within eight days and was not to come within half a mile of the town jurisdiction because she was known to have committed adultery with men other than her husband and she was also badly behaved and lived immorally, and was involved in facilitating illegal sexual acts.[84]

Nonetheless, it is clear that one of the aggravating circumstances for receiving harsher punishments was the simple circumstance of one's sex. As said, of 37 banishments that were imposed in the *Liber Causarum*, 27 were imposed on women, mainly for sexual offences, whereas only 2 men were banished for such offences. To this must be added, though, that more women were brought before the court for procuring and for a combination of prostitution and adultery, as well as for five unknown, probably sexual offences (as for all of them a banishment was imposed).[85] This suggests that they were more regularly denounced than men, which may indicate a lower threshold for the disapproval of immoral behaviour of women.[86] As such, they were also more likely to be ousted for such offences. But women were also banished six times for adultery, whereas only one man was punished that way, despite the fact that a practically equal amount of men and women was charged with this offence.[87] This stricter punishment of women for adultery matches penal practices elsewhere, such as that in Konstanz, where women were often judged to have had a more active role than men.[88] In medieval Ulm, there had also been an increased focus on sexual morality, but the issue was only taken up systematically after the Reformation. This resulted in an increase in punishment of sexual offenders, especially through banishment. The majority of women banished had been charged with immoral behaviour.[89] It also appears that the Kampen town council became stricter towards

[84] LC, f. 6r (8 Oct 1476).

[85] According to the *Liber Causarum*, 45 women and 29 men were charged with adultery and/or facilitating prostitution or illegal sexual acts (including the five unknown sexual offences) between 1474 and 1500.

[86] Lipscomb, *Voices of Nîmes*, 89–90, 147–52, points to the importance of female networks and resulting gossip in the identification and prosecution of immoral behaviour, especially of women, in the Protestant consistory courts in Languedoc. Whether women were denouncing women in Kampen is unclear.

[87] A total of 27 men and 26 women appeared in court on a charge of adultery according to the *Liber Causarum* (1474–1500).

[88] Schuster, *Stadt vor Gericht*, 115–8.

[89] Coy, *Strangers and Misfits*, 65.

facilitating prostitution and adultery in the fourth quarter of the fifteenth century. In the third quarter nobody was banished for holding 'bad inns' alone, whereas in the fourth quarter a number of people, mainly women, received this penalty for bringing together married people or women and priests for illegal sexual acts, such as Alijt Koggenstuers who was charged with holding a 'bad inn' and keeping married people away from each other. She was sentenced to a five-year banishment, a relatively long period.[90] It is also noticeable that the number of men banished in the *Digestum Vetus* (1454–1473) and the *Liber Causarum* (1475–1500) was the same, whereas that of women increased from 6 in the *Digestum Vetus* to 27 in the *Liber Causarum*.

The fact that women were more often banished than men for sexual crimes may have been due to the fact that women were traditionally seen as the guilty party when it came to sexual offences.[91] Also, in some cases of adultery the man probably had a higher status than the woman. As we have seen, some men had relations with their female servants. People with a lower social status would sooner be banished (and indeed, sometimes only the woman was banished in cases of adultery). People of higher status could also more easily afford to pay a fine. Another economic reason can perhaps also be given: the men would in general be working in a profession and had a family to provide for. As such, any banishment of a man would be detrimental to the whole household. In Amsterdam, female breadwinners were not sentenced to banishment for that exact same reason.[92]

The increase in banishments for crimes against morality fits in with a general development in the later middle ages and leading up to the Reformation. In this period, there was a strong urban movement advocating public decency which was fuelled by the activities of Observant preachers like Bernardino of Siena and the already mentioned Brugman. It is probably no coincidence that by-laws regulating adultery and procuring

[90] LC, f. 45v (between 15 July and 17 October 1497). In Konstanz, too, magistrates dealt more strictly with morally offensive behaviour in the second half of the fifteenth century. Schuster, *Stadt vor Gericht*, 118.

[91] See, for example, Cohen, *Crossroads of Justice*, 85, 94–5; Crawford, *European Sexualities*, 172; Schuster, 'Hinaus oder ins Frauenhaus', 21; concerning concupiscence as associated with feminine nature, see Lansing, 'Gender and civic authority', 33, 40–5. See also the incarceration for sexual misconduct of women in early modern Marseille as analysed by Cattelona, 'Control and collaboration'.

[92] Boomgaard, *Misdaad en straf in Amsterdam*, 216. See also Berents, *Het werk van de vos*, 52–55; Brand and Frankot, 'Das Kampener Stadtbuch', 54.

were promulgated less than two months after Brugman's first visit. There also appears to have been an increase in the prosecution of sexual crimes, though there are few sources from before 1455 to confirm there was a change.[93] This morality movement was supported, or even initiated, by the members of the public, who were relied upon to bring forward complaints. According to the by-laws, those bringing charges would receive half the fine if the accused was convicted (and indeed in 1461 there were two people who received a quarter of the fine each in a case of adultery[94]). In addition, there is regular mention in the sources of complaints made by neighbours.[95] The increase in prosecution was most likely largely the result of an increase in denunciations which indicate a growing focus on morality among certain groups in society. Initially, in the decades directly following Brugman's visits, many of the accused got away with a warning. It was only in the last quarter of the fifteenth century that there appears to have been an increase in punitive measures against female offenders especially.[96] This was perhaps the result of increasingly clear signals from those who denounced their neighbours, that certain behaviour would no longer be tolerated. As studies of early modern towns such as Ulm and Augsburg have shown, the prosecution of immoral behaviour became more systematic after the Reformation.[97] Moreover, honourable men and especially women found a new arena to showcase their concerns about immoral behaviour in the Protestant consistory courts, as Lipscomb has shown with regard to the Languedoc.[98] In late medieval Kampen, the increase in banishments of women accused of immoral behaviour in the final quarter of the fifteenth century suggests a change in the perception of such acts among the magistracy, who in the previous quarter most likely already had had to deal with a growing number of denunciations. By the final

[93] There are three lists of sexual offenders in the *Digestum Vetus*, for example, two of which are from the 1460s and one which is undated. DV, f. 21a (n.d.), f. 47a (1462), f. 78b (1468).

[94] DV, f. 44v (30 March 1461).

[95] See also Brand and Frankot, 'Das Kampener Stadtbuch', 57–9. In early modern Ulm, denunciation was expected, and people could even be reprimanded for failing to do their civic duty. But most people were happy to cooperate with the local authorities in order to maintain a godly order. Coy, *Strangers and Misfits*, 63, 86, 116.

[96] Cf. Brand and Frankot, 'Das Kampener Stadtbuch', 59.

[97] Coy, *Strangers and Misfits*, 65; Tyler, 'Refugees and reform', 86.

[98] Lipscomb, *Voices of Nîmes*. The special role of women in policing women's behaviour has also been noted by Cattelona, 'Control and Collaboration', concerning early modern Marseille.

quarter of the century, they became more prepared to also start sentencing more strictly.

This period also saw an increase in the focus on morality in the language used in the legal records.[99] When comparing the *Digestum Vetus* and the *Liber Causarum*, there is a notable difference in the use of adjectives denoting acceptable and unacceptable behaviour and language. Words like 'oneerlike' (dishonourable), 'quellike' (unruly), 'myslike' (unreliable), 'quade' (bad), 'onhoefflike' (discourteous), 'schantelike' (shameful), 'onwijslike' (unwise), 'onredelike' (unreasonable), 'onbehoirlike' (improper) and 'onrustelike' (restless) are used more regularly in the *Liber Causarum* and are opposed to 'vredelike' (peaceful), 'rustlike' (calm), 'hoeffsche' (courteous), 'guede' (good), 'eerlike' (honest), 'sedichlike' (virtuous) and similar terms. For example, Grete Holle was said to live in a restless, dishonourable and unruly fashion with her neighbours, arguing, speaking ill and using dishonourable, discourteous and disgraceful words against them, calling and insulting them. She was warned against all of this and told to stop her inappropriate behaviour ('onmanierlicheit') as the council would no longer tolerate it and preferred to see her leave ('wil sie hier niet langer liden').[100] Dyrck up die Sluse had been behaving indecently, visiting other women at night and frequenting disreputable taverns ('oneerlijken herbergen'). In addition, he was living with his wife in a restless and unruly fashion, and he was hitting her. He was told to stop his indecent and dishonourable behaviour and live quietly and peacefully with his wife as he should ('als dat behoirt').[101] Other husbands (and an occasional wife) were also warned to 'do as a good husband (or wife) should do to his wife (her husband)'.[102] Melijs Buth, finally, who was sentenced to be banished for two years, was charged with general misbehaviour: becoming increasingly more 'boeffliken en de schalckliken' (disgraceful or evil and bad or sinful), not making any effort to be good ('tot gienre doecht en schickt') and not obeying the good men who tried to council him.[103] The absence of any specific offences is particularly notable in this case, especially considering his severe punishment.

[99] Concerning language in legal records and how it expressed perceptions, see also McIntosh, 'Finding language for misconduct' (pointing to an influx of unmarried outsiders perceived as threatening social order as an explanation for a change in language in market centre courts in the second half of the fifteenth century—p. 112); Hanawalt, 'Good governance', 248; Gauvard, *'De Grace Especial'*, 111–43.

[100] LC, f. 18v (July 1484).

[101] LC, f. 25v (20 June 1488).

[102] For example, LC, f. 14r: 'doen als en guet man bij sijnen wijve schuldich is toe doene'.

[103] LC, f. 24r (26 November 1487).

In addition to the use of legal terminology that is focused on morality, there is also an increase in cases in which behaviour, including the use of particular language, is considered to be offensive and worthy of punishment (or at least a warning in court). The wording 'soe en wil men sie hier inder stat niet lijden', moreover, confirms that offensive and immoral behaviour could ultimately lead to exclusion from the community. Worth noting in this context are certain comments on the effect that certain behaviour and language had on the good people of the town, or on the culprits' neighbours. For example, in 1492 Femme mitten Tanden's behaviour was said to sadden all good people and the neighbours ('soe dattet allen gueden luden ende den nabueren verdriet').[104]

This supports the view already noted that the magistrates and the 'good people' of Kampen agreed on what was considered to be acceptable, honourable behaviour and that these good people expected the magistrates to take action. Occasionally, the magistrates can be seen to go beyond what was expected of them: in 1459, in a case of a man who treated his mother unreasonably, a note is included that perhaps his mother was willing to tolerate such behaviour, but that the council most certainly was not ('al woldet die moeder van hem lijden, die raet wils in geenrewijs van hem lijden').[105] Also, the magistrates can occasionally be seen to be prepared to punish miscreants more harshly than was detailed in the by-laws. Moye Geert in 1482 would, on continuing his misbehaviour, not be punished according to the 'gemene kuer' as others were, but in the sharpest way, on the decision of the aldermen.[106] Such individually decided punishments ('ter scepen claringe') were also regularly said to act as an 'example' that is to say that they were expected to act as a deterrent. Through its practice of punishment and warning, the magistrates were thus explicitly communicating a message to the general population with regard to behaviour that could lead to exclusion.

Overall, it appears, then, that relatively many women were banished as a primary punishment. The behaviours that led to banishment from urban society, such as adultery and procuring, were those that were especially associated with women. In addition, women were more likely to be considered the guilty party in sexual crimes, and they were seen as less vital to

[104] LC, f. 35r (August 1492).
[105] DV, f. 32r (15 February 1459).
[106] LC, f. 13r (between 24 September and 12 November 1482).

the urban economy. The vast majority of exiles were, however, men, as they were much more likely to be caught up in violent episodes, and because violence incurred the highest fines.

## The Role of Social Class

The assessment of the role of social class in punishment is more difficult than that of gender, because it is often difficult, if not impossible, to gain social information on the offenders that feature in the sources. The profession of miscreants is only mentioned in some of the cases and last names may or may not provide clues about someone's activities. In some cases, someone's last name equates with their profession, but in other cases it does not.[107] Similarly, toponymic surnames may or may not indicate a person's place of origin or residence. As a result, it is difficult to confirm whether such a person was a Kampen inhabitant or citizen or not. The citizenship administration is only extant until 1469.

Nonetheless, it is possible to draw some conclusions from the available material. In some cases, a person's description includes both a surname and a profession or a place name (or both). In the *oerveden* registers only very few entries include a profession (about one in nine). These are mostly craftsmen, particularly fullers and weavers, but also the executioner and a sexton. Professions are named about twice as often in the banishment register. There, too, many are craftsmen, but there is also a significant group of servants. Weavers and fullers again appear regularly, as do millers, tailors and smiths. These may well represent relatively large groups of Kampen society, which had a modest textile industry, but it is noteworthy that there is only one baker, when there are ten millers.[108] On the other hand, as we do not have information on more than 75 per cent of the offenders, there are no major conclusions to be drawn on the use of

[107] For example, Goesen Holtsaeger (Wood sawyer) had two men standing surety for him, both called Tymmerman (Carpenter). Reg, p. 415 (1497). In that case, it is likely, though not definitely true, that all three names indicate a profession, as a wood sawyer would normally have had carpenters in his professional network. Johan Pelser, on the other hand, was not a furrier, as his name might suggest, but a fuller ('vulre'). Reg, p. 390 (1486).

[108] Weavers displaying disobedience also appeared prominently in the early modern Ulm records. Coy, *Strangers and Misfits*, 64. In fourteenth-century Zürich, tailors and millers are also regularly mentioned, as are shoemakers and butchers. Burghartz, *Leib, Ehre und Gut*, 100. Zaremska (*Les bannis au Moyen Âge*, 139) also notes the prominence of craftsmen and servants among the accused (and the victims) of violence.

violence among groups of craftsmen (and their lacking ability to pay the relevant fines for this violence).

At least a quarter of offenders in the *oerveden* register was not originally from Kampen. This should not come as a surprise, as people from elsewhere were more likely to be put in custody and made to swear not to harm the town, because they would have had more difficulty in securing people who could stand surety for them. There are far fewer entries that include places of origin outside of Kampen in the banishment register. Seeing that the latter is generally more informative concerning its offenders, it is likely that relatively more offenders in the *oerveden* register were from out of town than in the banishment register.

In other cases, it is clear that someone was from Kampen, for example because a spouse is mentioned who also fell under the Kampen jurisdiction. For example, Maye, the wife of Willem Riemslager, was initially given grace from banishment (for adultery) because her husband declared himself willing to forgive her, and she was allowed to remain with him in Kampen. She was ultimately banished after all, after having been facilitated by three other women to lie with a clergyman in the bathhouse and bordellos during Lent. However, it is clear from the entry that she was a Kampen inhabitant. Judging by his name, her husband may have been a beltmaker.[109]

A number of the women who were banished also had toponymic surnames, or placenames attached to their names. Like with toponymics for men, it is not clear whether these women actually came from elsewhere. It is notable, however, that these women were not identified by either a husband or a father's name, like many of the other women in the sources were. So, they may well have been immigrants whose main point of identification was their origin, such as Lamme and Aelheit of Groningen, Lijse and Heyle of Nijmegen, Bethkyn Vos of Zutphen, Gertruidt of Essen and Griete of Bremen. Only one of these seven women was definitely married.

It is difficult to assess whether or not a woman's status as a married or unmarried woman affected their punishment. In fact, it is likely that in two cases, their marriage was actually a deteriorating factor in the sentencing of two women: Nase and Mette in 1474 and 1477 respectively were told to join their husbands who were already in exile.[110] It may well be that these women had resorted to (facilitating) prostitution to make ends meet

[109] LC, f. 28v (April 1490); Reg, p. 22 (1490).
[110] LC, f. 2r (13 October 1474); LC, f. 7r (22 November 1477).

after their husbands' banishment. In the case of Maye, Willem Riemslager's wife (see earlier), however, her husband's mercy saved her from exile initially. It may well be that a husband's willingness to show such mercy was an important factor in the decision whether or not to banish women who had been charged with adultery or other sexual crimes. In early modern Ulm, the wishes of a wronged spouse were also known to influence the sentencing.[111] But there were also unmarried women who only received a warning, such as Quade Derixken, whose nickname 'Quade' suggests she had a bad reputation. She was charged with facilitating illegal sexual acts in December of 1475 and given a warning. She was ultimately banished after continued complaints from her neighbours, but that was not until April 1479.[112] The before mentioned Ghertruidt of Essen was also given a warning after she had been found to live dishonourably with a priest in 1497.[113] Maiken, on the other hand, who was said to be living with Willem van Essen, was banished in 1481.[114] Unlike unmarried women, unmarried men were unlikely to be charged with sexual offences unless these were 'against nature', such as homosexual acts or bestiality. As such, an unmarried status was not a major factor in the banishment of males for immoral acts. Nonetheless, it is likely that a married man was considered differently by the court, because he had other responsibilities and was expected to act more responsibly. This can be expected to have affected his punishment both positively and negatively.

It is unclear whether a person's status as a burgher had any influence on their punishment or on the magistrates' perception of them. There is no specific mention of individuals' status as a citizen in relation to any verdicts or punishments, so we cannot establish either a positive or negative effect of this status. In addition, it is often difficult to determine whether someone was a citizen or not. The *Burgerboek* includes mainly names, many of them patronymics, and it is virtually impossible to link most of these to individuals that appear elsewhere in the sources. Either people had very common names, or they had non-patronymic aliases that were not noted in the *Burgerboek*.[115] For early modern Ulm, Coy was able to differentiate between citizens, resident aliens and vagrants. Citizens tended to be

[111] Coy, *Strangers and Misfits*, 96.
[112] LC, f. 4v.
[113] LC, f. 46r.
[114] LC, f. 11r.
[115] For example, there are 12 Henric Henricsz and 18 Johan Johansz/Jansz.

treated leniently initially. For adultery, for example, they received an eight-day imprisonment and a verbal reprimand, but their conviction did not result in permanent dishonour. Instead, the magistrates aimed to save the marriage. Overall, citizens were much less likely to be banished than migrants and vagrants. Of citizens sentenced, only 26 per cent were ordered to leave town, against 37 per cent of resident aliens and 82 per cent of vagrants. Migrants were also subject to stricter laws from 1527, especially concerning their fiscal and moral obligations. As a result of an economic downturn, the town had no qualms in ousting non-citizens who threatened the town's prosperity or morality.[116]

Usually, the only individuals in Kampen we can be certain were citizens are the members of some of the elite families, or the magistrates themselves. There were, for example, three members of the Van Uterwijc family who were banished in 1482 (Ruederic), 1493 (Herman) and 1496 (Wolter) respectively, all three for a wounding at night.[117] Only Ruederic and Wolter appear to have returned to Kampen and Wolter may be the same as the man that functioned as alderman and councillor between 1505 and 1519. In 1479, Peter van Uterwijc, the son of the castellan of nearby castle Kuinre, also paid off a high fine.[118] Johan Coipsz, who was an alderman and councillor between 1485 and 1494, was reprimanded by his colleagues on the council for improper conduct with women and 'ander deernen', probably prostitutes, and indiscreet and underhanded talk. They also suspected him of talking about council business outside the council ('dat hie nyet yn rade solde holden dat rait is'). They gave him a stern warning that he would be thrown off the council if his conduct would not improve.[119] In this case, it may be that Coipsz's status as a magistrate actually exacerbated matters; his behaviour shamed his colleagues. It is possible that his conduct eventually led to Coipsz's departure from the council a year later. Some years earlier, another councillor had also been reprimanded by his colleagues for using improper language in the council and on the street. He was warned to act more honourably in the future, or the council would punish him as they should and as they had previously penalised other council members.[120]

[116] Coy, *Strangers and Misfits*, 58, 60, 68, 74.
[117] Reg, p. 141, 143, 149.
[118] Reg, p. 383.
[119] LC, f. 36r (14 February 1493).
[120] LC, f. 26r (14 August 1488).

So, members of Kampen's elite certainly did not escape justice, and they too might have ended up banished. It is probable that the three members of the Van Uterwijc family were all young men who did not have access to enough money to pay off the large fines set for woundings. In addition, their relatives might have wanted to teach them a lesson by not footing the bill for them, or at least not immediately. As evidence from Italian communes unearthed by Carol Lansing has also suggested, the elite were certainly not averse to breaking the laws they themselves helped to create, and then to prosecute themselves.[121] In the cases of Ernst Witte and Johan Coipsz, the magistrates may have been genuinely ashamed of their colleagues (as well as concerned that their secrets would be advertised to anyone willing to listen), but they also needed to be seen calling on them to answer for their behaviour. In order to be taken seriously as keepers of a morally pure social order, the magistrates needed to also control their own conduct, and punish those that threatened their status and prestige.

## Ceremony and Symbolism

There is very little evidence concerning any symbolic rituals that accompanied the expulsion of offenders from Kampen. Nothing is mentioned in the by-laws, though this is not unusual in a European context. As Gerd Althoff has argued, secular rituals tended to be flexible; medieval political actors 'varied, mixed, or updated them in keeping with the given situation or even invented new rituals'.[122] As such, descriptions of rituals did not necessarily find their way into normative texts. In Kampen, some of the only clues are provided by two cases in the *Digestum Vetus*. In these, warnings were given to the accused (both of them women). Wolbrich was told to leave the town between her trial (17 August 1471) and Christmas Eve of the same year and remain at a distance of at least one mile. If she would not leave during this time, she would be escorted out of town by the executioner banging on a cymbal ('mit eenen becken cloppende'), while she would be made to wear a green wreath on her head.[123] Her offences had been that she lived apart from her husband, in adultery, had children

[121] Lansing, *Passion and Order*, 2.

[122] Althoff, 'The variability of rituals', 73. In Scotland the form in which banishments were carried out was not regulated either. Ewan, 'Crossing borders and boundaries', 245.

[123] It is unclear what the green wreath was meant to symbolise.

annually and was facilitating prostitution.[124] A similar warning was given to Jutte van Bronnepe who had been asked to leave the town immediately for insulting good men and women, generally ungodly living, procuring and fornication with priests, married men and other 'honourable' men.[125] From this it appears that the women were allowed to leave Kampen of their own accord, Wolbrich even being allowed four months to prepare for her departure. Only if they refused to leave, were they to be subjected to a demeaning ritual. It is questionable then that this ritual was conducted on a regular basis when banishment was the main punishment.

This picture is confirmed when we analyse the other cases in which someone was banished as a primary punishment. In the majority of these cases, the culprits were given a deadline by which they had to leave Kampen, suggesting that they could organise their departure themselves. Usually, this was a defined period within a two-week period. Of 28 banishments in the *Liber Causarum*, 9 had to leave town within 8 days, 7 within 3 days, 2 each within 1, 4 and 14 days and 1 within 5 days.[126] One person had to leave immediately, one was given 28 days, and in three cases the deadline is not indicated. In some of these entries a date is mentioned by which the exiles had to have left, in others a number of days within which they needed to depart. In the *Digestum Vetus* the deadline is not mentioned as often as in the *Liber Causarum*. On a few occasions, people were told to leave 'bij schinender sonne', that is before sunset.[127] In this context, the four months granted to Wolbrich appear even more generous. Similar spaces of time were found by Maurer for medieval German towns: most commonly until sundown on the same day, 3, 8 or 14 days, and occasionally several weeks.[128] So there, too, many offenders were able to arrange their own departure. That not everyone left Kampen without any kind of supervision or accompaniment is suggested by a note from 1488 concerning Bette, the 'deerne' of Lambert the 'calckberner' (lime burner), who had returned illegally after having been turned out of

[124] DV, f. 115r (17 August 1471).

[125] DV, f. 119v (14 December 1471). It should be noted that the men apparently continued to be 'honourable' despite the fornication—the woman was considered to be the seductress.

[126] For example, LC, f. 2r (1474; within three days), f. 24v (1488; within eight days).

[127] For example, DV, f. 34r (27 September 1459), f. 72r (3 March 1470).

[128] Maurer, 'Erzwungene Ferne', 202.

the town by a town official ('boeven dat sie myt enen stat diener wt der stadt gewijst was').[129]

So, instead of being whipped out of the city upon sentencing, as appeared to have been the norm in many cases in sixteenth-century Ulm (though not in Augsburg at the same time) most Kampen exiles were given some time to put their affairs in order, pack their bags and say their goodbyes.[130] Also, instead of being seen off by a potentially malicious crowd, culprits were able to leave quietly, perhaps escorted only by friends and loved ones. Allowing exiles to leave of their own accord meant that the magistrates surrendered an opportunity to display their power and their commitment maintaining public order. It might be that they had found different ways of making examples of outcasts, for example by publicly announcing their expulsion from Kampen in a symbolic place, but there is no specific evidence of this. In addition, this alternative is unlikely to have been a spectacle like a scourging through the streets which it would have been difficult for the onlookers to forget.

A public spectacle was very occasionally staged, it seems: in 1497 three men were cast out of town ('sijn wt der stat gekloept') as a result of violence. This is the only other case in which the term 'cloppen' was used in the context of a banishment. The men had come to the house of Johan Backer (the baker) and banged on the glass window where his wife was lying-in, five or six days after having given birth. She called her husband, afraid that they were trying to kill her. The men repeatedly demanded that Johan come out of his house, while in the meantime they broke the planks of the window where he normally laid out his bread.[131] The behaviour of the three men was obviously considered to have been such a serious breach of the peace that they were banished with a public ritual. One of the men was allowed to return in 1505 on payment of 25 gold guilders. It is unclear what the ritual consisted of exactly, but their expulsion was clearly accompanied by noise ('cloppen') which would have alerted Kampen's inhabitants to the proceedings.

In the vast majority of cases there is no mention of any rituals accompanying the banishment. As is clear from the examples presented earlier, it is not that the Kampen magistrates did not use any displays in their punishment practices at all. There were several ways in which punishments could

[129] Reg, p. 137.
[130] Hoffmann, 'Der Stadtverweis', 224.
[131] Reg, p. 151 (1497).

be made to carry an added symbolic weight. Johan Jansz, who took back his confession of theft, had originally been sentenced to wearing a noose as a symbol of having been granted mercy from hanging, possibly while he was being banished, as was already detailed in Chap. 3. This symbolic gesture is also illustrated in the image accompanying the entry (see Fig. 3.5).[132] This symbol was, however, related to his crime of theft, for which the punishment was hanging, and not to the banishment. There is no evidence either that any ceremonies took place when an exile was allowed to return to the town, though, of course, the lack of evidence does not rule out that they did. For the town council it was mainly important to note down in its registers who owed it money and who had paid, which warnings were given and to whom and who was banished and on what conditions. These were issues that needed to be recorded and remembered as they needed continued execution and monitoring.[133] It was much less important to record that a ritual or ceremony had taken place as this did not have any relevance for future dealings with a convict.

Rituals were used elsewhere in Europe when people were banished. In early modern Dundee in Scotland, for example, a female offender was 'scourged about the burgh, with the bellman ringing the hand bell, declaring her offence', after which she was branded on the cheek at the market cross and banished. Others, however, were simply cast out without any rituals.[134] In medieval London, prostitutes on their third conviction were publicly shorn before being taken to a city gate and cast out of the community.[135] In medieval Lyon, the condemned were made to follow a set route, including a stop at the pillory. There the culprits were flogged, before being eventually escorted out. Along this route were a number of points representing civic and ecclesiastical power.[136] Similar routes were followed in medieval Polish towns.[137] In early modern Ulm, male vagrants were exposed at the pillory and flogged through the streets before being cast out of the city.[138] Many of the entries in the town's punishment books ('Urgichten') were even accompanied by graphic illustrations showing the

[132] DV, f. 18v (15 July 1455).

[133] See also Zaremska, *Les bannis au Moyen Âge*, 127.

[134] Ewan, 'Crossing borders and boundaries', 245.

[135] Hanawalt, 'Rituals of inclusion and exclusion', 27.

[136] Zaremska, *Les bannis au Moyen Âge*, 83.

[137] Ibid., 183; Jeziorski, 'Die Strafe der Ausweisung', 37.

[138] Coy, 'Beggars at the gates', 620. Women were subjected to less physically painful forms of public humiliation. Ibid., 633.

convicted, sometimes with bare upper bodies, being chased by a running executioner with a birch bundle.[139] In early modern Augsburg, too, corporal punishment and rituals of shaming preceded some banishments.[140] Of course, in Kampen, too, some of the delinquents were flogged before they were banished, but it is not clear from the sources whether the flogging was considered to be a separate punishment, or that it was a shaming ritual that was attached to the banishment. There is no sign that offenders were flogged through the streets while they were being escorted out. In fact, the entries normally specify that the culprits were flogged at the 'stupe', the pillory. For example, in 1450, Lentien, the son of Peter Claesz, swore an *oervede* oath because he had been in prison, and he was flogged at the pillory as well as banned from coming within five miles of the town.[141] Thirteen others were similarly punished between 1447 and 1500. A few others were branded or mutilated in addition to being banished ensuring their dishonour would be recognised and remembered for the rest of their lives.[142] Most likely, though, the effect of the combination of flogging and casting out was the same in that the magistrates could showcase their dedication to social order by excluding particular lawbreakers from their midst in a public ritual that would ensure their offences and expulsion would be remembered by as many of the members of the community as possible.[143] It may be that the magistrates were careful in their decisions concerning who to make an example of. Those who were flogged before an expulsion were culprits who were considered to be dishonourable enough to be kept in custody before their conviction. They were mostly banished for life. The offenders who were allowed to arrange their own departure, on the other hand, were women and men denounced for immoral behaviour. Most of them were expected to return to Kampen in due course. At a time when offenders convicted of immoral acts had perhaps only recently started to be banished, the magistrates may not have been prepared to turn their punishment into a spectacle by flogging them through the streets.

In the western and southern Netherlands, it was common to send offenders on a punitive pilgrimage as an alternative to banishment.

[139] Coy, *Strangers and Misfits*, 130, plus figures on 13, 48 (birch bundle only), 78, 131.
[140] Tyler, 'Refugees and reform', 87.
[141] Reg, p. 2.
[142] For example, Reg, p. 4 (1453), p. 5 (1455), p. 14 (1476, p. 15 (1477).
[143] Coy, 'Beggars at the gates', 620; Coy, *Strangers and Misfits*, Ch. 5. See also concerning punishment as a process rather than as a single act Geltner, *Flogging Others*, 25.

Pilgrimages had a symbolic function in that these journeys were meant to purify the lawbreaker as a sinner. Pilgrimages also gave exiles a purpose and as such could be considered more merciful than outright banishment (though a pilgrimage could be equally, if not more dangerous). A pilgrimage also had the added benefit to the town that the exile could not cause any problems on its periphery during their expulsion.[144] But pilgrimages were not common in the eastern Netherlands (or elsewhere in Europe) and the Kampen court only sentenced a small amount of people to pilgrimages from 1500 onwards, at a time when elsewhere, especially in the western Netherlands in the fifteenth and sixteenth centuries, pilgrimages were slowly being replaced by other penalties.[145]

Overall, then, the Kampen magistrates do not appear to have sought to add symbolic meaning to the act of physically excluding offenders from the town community as a rule, though some offenders were flogged preceding mostly permanent banishments. In order to be able to receive any assistance from the town inhabitants in executing and maintaining banishments, these inhabitants did need to be informed about who was banished and who was allowed to return. It is for the purposes of communication and to stress the complicity of judges and public opinion that rituals and symbolism were especially useful.[146] Lacking these, there must have been other mechanisms in place. It may be that lists of banished offenders were read out regularly, for example by a town crier or during church services. The town employed a horn blower, who was to blow his horn on all street corners when ordered to do so and when people were taken into custody.[147] It seems likely that his services were also used to announce who had

[144] Van Herwaarden, *Opgelegde bedevaarten*, 25, 405; Glaudemans, *Om die wrake wille*, 185.

[145] Two Kampen examples are known to me from the first years of the sixteenth century: LC, f. 52r (3 December 1500); f. 68v (20 February 1505), the latter offering the offender a choice between banishment and pilgrimage. No research was conducted beyond 1505. With regard to penal pilgrimages being replaced in the western Netherlands, see Van Herwaarden, *Opgelegde bedevaarten*, 27. In Dordrecht, for example, the imposing of pilgrimages was significantly reduced in 1400. Van Herwaarden, *Opgelegde bedevaarten*, 297.

[146] Concerning the transmitting of messages about inclusion and exclusion through rituals, see also Coy, 'Beggars at the gates', 620; Coy, *Strangers and Misfits*, 26, 81, 120–2; Ewan, 'Crossing borders and boundaries', 245; Gauvard in Zaremska, *Les bannis au Moyen Âge*, 10; Hawes, 'The urban community', 365–6, 379.

[147] LD, f. 195v; Tamboer and Van Vlisteren, 'Medieval ban horn?', 224 and figure 18. There are also annual payments to the horn blower in the town account, for example, SR, f. 180r (1490).

been banished and who had fled from justice. This, combined with the physical expulsion, appears to have generally served the magistrates' objectives of excluding specific offenders from the community and communicating their commitment to maintaining a moral society.[148] The maintenance of law and social control more generally was communicated through penal practices such as shameful punishments, floggings, mutilations and capital punishments.

## An Army of Exiles?

So, without a purpose like a journey to a saint's shrine, where did the 26–27 people who were banished from the town of Kampen on an annual basis go or what happened to them? From studies of other cities, we know that groups of exiles sometimes hung around just outside the walls or outside the freedom and that it was difficult to monitor and police outcasts returning to the city. In Ulm in the second half of the sixteenth century, for example, stricter laws were issued to act as a deterrent against exiles entering the town, but to little avail.[149] In medieval Ghent there are indications that exiles caused some unrest just beyond the town bounds.[150] Similar problems were reported in medieval Dordrecht and Alkmaar.[151] Throughout Europe, groups of vagrants were considered to be causing trouble and were viewed with increasing suspicion by the authorities and by people more generally. Travellers felt unsafe along certain routes, such as the mountainous and forested regions in Eastern Europe.[152] Of course, many of these vagrants may have been exiles trying to make a life for themselves without the protection of a static community. Even those who were banished temporarily could be faced with real hardship. They might have been able to enter other cities during daytime, but some towns had by-

[148] In medieval Fritzlar, too, magistrates made sure banishments were communicated widely. Von Brockdorf, 'Die Strafe des Stadtverweises', 48.

[149] Ulm's policy was mainly aimed at vagrants who, in the economic downturn of this period, flocked to the city. They were increasingly prosecuted and banished, but it proved difficult to prevent them from returning. In addition, 'unruly shanty towns' rose just outside the town walls. Coy, 'Beggars at the gates', 626–8. See also Berents, *Misdaad in de Middeleeuwen*, 49–50; Berents, *Het werk van de vos*, 80. Coy, *Strangers and Misfits*, 31–56.

[150] Van Eetveld, 'Vrouwencriminaliteit', 10. Seeing that Ghent banishments were apparently valid for the whole of Flanders, this suggests that monitoring was a real issue.

[151] Glaudemans, *Om die wrake wille*, 199.

[152] Glaudemans, *Om die wrake wille*, 199, 204, 206; Zaremska, *Les bannis au Moyen Âge*, 101.

laws against 'foreign' exiles staying overnight. They had to leave town before sundown.[153] A captured exile in Zeeland reported in 1502 that he had slept mostly in fields and meadows for the past two years, and only very rarely in houses and on beds.[154] Others might have been able to stay with friends or family. For some, a banishment might just have been another stage in their migratory life. Zaremska has asked to what extent exile was an actual punishment when so many in urban society came from elsewhere and a life of mobility was fairly normal. In Avignon, in the second quarter of the fourteenth century, for example, about three-quarters of the population consisted of newcomers.[155] How successful an individual was in making a new life for themselves after a banishment depended on different factors, such as character, background and age, but also on the economic viability of the region they were living in. In general, though, it is difficult to get a clear picture about the activities and whereabouts of exiles.

In Kampen there is some evidence that people returned to town before their banishment was up. First of all, there are the by-laws which concern returned exiles which were discussed in Chap. 2: in 1334 it was laid down that people who fled or were exiled because of an unpaid fine and were caught within the town or freedom after their banishment should be fined 80 lb. For those who had been ousted from the community for debts it was half the fine. Anyone assisting exiles by offering them a place to stay was meted out the same penalty.[156] In the second half of the fifteenth century, there were obviously some problems with returning exiles, as in 1479 when the town offered anyone who arrested an outcast, or was instrumental in their arrest, half the fine, that is to say 40 lb. for catching anyone due a fine.[157] For exiles who were 'only' flogged or otherwise punished corporally on their return, the town would pay the informer 10 lb. The oath of the bridgemaster, recorded in 1466, also included the promise that he would inform the burgomasters of any exiles crossing the bridge in either direction.[158]

[153] Berents, *Het werk van de vos*, 80.

[154] Glaudemans, *Om die wrake wille*, 197.

[155] Zaremska, *Les bannis au Moyen Âge*, 84, 171.

[156] GB, f. 42v. In Valenciennes, people could be banished themselves for helping others. Huart, 'Maintenir la paix', 15.

[157] DN, f. 31r (1479). The promise of half the fine was also included in some other by-laws.

[158] DN, f. 12r. The bridge across the IJssel was built in 1448.

The register of banishments also includes some evidence that on occasion exiles returned to the town before their fines were paid. Thirty-three entries, all dated between 1451 and 1492, have annotations concerning additional fines for unauthorised returns to Kampen. In accordance with the by-laws, 80 lb. was added to their existing fines with the exception of Diric Gijsbertsz who had been banished for debt and, again following the regulations, was charged with an extra 40 lb.[159] Five of the exiles had been spotted twice and as a result had 160 lb. added to their fine. The bridgemasters caught at least some of the offenders: on three occasions (all after the above mentioned 1466 by-law) it is noted that the outcasts were seen (or caught) on the bridge.[160]

It is difficult to say whether these 33 offenders were just the tip of the iceberg. Without a police force, it would have been difficult to monitor the return of any exiles, especially outside the gates in the freedom. The bridgemaster and the watchmen by the gates (who are also said to have caught offenders on three occasions)[161] would have kept an eye out, as did the aldermen who apparently spotted an exile in the town freedom in 1488.[162] Obviously, though, it was possible to enter the town unobserved, as most offenders were caught inside the town walls. Some were even caught in very public spaces, such as St Mary's church, the town cellar and one of the town's taverns.[163] It is likely, then, that many turned a blind eye when they spotted an exile. The 1479 by-law suggests that the magistrates realised that more exiles were returning than they would be able to catch and that they needed help from inhabitants in policing returning outcasts. How they came to this conclusion remains the question (perhaps they noticed that exiles' goods were secretly removed),[164] but it is unlikely that they would have issued a by-law if less than one exile returned to the city unauthorised every year. This also suggests that the magistrates had trouble convincing the inhabitants to cooperate in catching these men and women. It was important, then, to be able to depend on the men guarding the gates. In seventeenth-century Augsburg, exiles were taken to all

[159] Reg, p. 82 (1449).

[160] Reg, p. 108 (1467), p. 118 (1472), p. 119 (1472).

[161] Reg, p. 103 (1464), p. 129 (1482), p. 137 (1488).

[162] Reg, p. 137 (1488).

[163] Respectively: Reg, p. 91 (1454): p. 130 (1483); LC, f. 27r (1489).

[164] This is suggested by the issuing of by-laws in 1470 and 1477 forbidding the removal or hiding of goods discussed above. Only one person was charged with assisting an exile in removing his goods at night. Reg, p. 101 (1462).

the gates so the gatekeepers could take a good look at them.[165] This may have been a common measure in medieval and early modern Europe and suggests that exiles returning was a problem that existed everywhere.

The fact that people took the risk of an additional 80 lb. fine also suggests that the chances of being caught were low and that they were likely being supported (or at least ignored) by many within the town. In some cases, though, people seemed especially unlucky. Jan Arntsz, for example, was banished for a mere 2 lb. in 1466, but saw 80 lb. added to this when he was spotted in Kampen.[166] The same happened to Tyman Luttike in 1462, on top of the 9 lb. he owed the town.[167] Despite this, Luttike subsequently managed to repay his debt and was allowed to return to join the town community. But one can only imagine that an 89 lb. fine would have taken a long time to settle for someone who had initially been unable to pay 9 lb. Johan Matthijsz, on the other hand, was already due to pay the enormous sum of 460 lb. in 1453 when he was caught inside the town freedom. His high fine was the result of a night of violence: he had gone out one night and had attacked a number of individuals, including a blind man who had the snares of his lute broken before he ended up with a bloody nose and mouth. Another 80 lb. was added when he returned to town. He too apparently managed to pay off his debt, as his entry has been crossed out (more regarding this in Chap. 5).[168] That a continued watch was out for people who had been registered as banished, becomes clear from the case of Johan Heymansz who was cast out of the town in 1459 for a fine for pulling the cape or coat off a brother of St Brigit. Heymansz returned four years later, in 1463, was recognised, and also had 80 lb. added to his fine.[169] A case which appears even more extraordinary is that of Evert Koster who was banished in 1480 for failing to pay a fine for the use of an illegal weapon. This entry states that he was caught in Kampen on two occasions: at Easter in the year 1500 and at *Visitationis* (2 July) in 1502.[170] The reason that he was caught, the second time at least, was that his wife had filed a complaint because he had broken open her door with

[165] Illegal returns were registered systematically in Augsburg from 1600. From this registration, it is clear that some exiles returned repeatedly. One individual was even caught 22 times. Hoffmann, 'Der Stadtverweis', 218, 221.

[166] Reg, p. 107 (1466).

[167] Reg, p. 101 (1462). The entry was crossed out.

[168] Reg, p. 86 (1453). The entry was crossed out.

[169] Reg, p. 97 (1459 (and 1463)).

[170] Reg, p. 128.

an axe which he had brought along. It appears, then, that Evert had never paid his fine and was still banished 22 years after he was cast out. In the meantime, his wife had remained in Kampen and had obviously been able to manage without him. It may well be that she only denounced him because he threatened her.

Besides the by-laws and notes on added fines in the banishment register, there is no evidence that the magistrates were concerned about any 'armies' of exiles on the borders of their town freedom.[171] Schuster, in his study of Konstanz, has suggested that outcasts were only able to keep up their social connections within the town if they were exiled for no more than a year or at a distance of a few miles. For this reason, offenders sentenced to banishments from Konstanz for longer than one year in particular tried to get these sentences converted to fines. Those who decided to leave the town after all tried to stay as close as possible, so as to be able to keep in touch with relatives and friends or even keep an eye on business where relevant.[172] But such exiles were not necessarily the ones the town magistrates would be concerned about. It was poor, unemployed folk without any connections that town councils in the middle ages and early modern period sought to keep out of their walled communities, such as the people flocking to the city of Ulm mentioned above. They were subsequently cast out when they became a burden and settled in the shanty towns around the walls.[173] Of course, such groups mainly became a burden when a town was in economic decline; growing cities like Amsterdam even welcomed those banished from elsewhere as long as they obeyed the law.[174]

It appears that the economic situation in Kampen was not as desperate as that in Ulm, at least not in the fifteenth century. It was not until the early sixteenth century that wars waged in the surrounding countryside might have led to an increase of fugitives in Kampen. On the other hand, there does appear to have been an increase in by-laws in the last quarter of

[171] Berents, *Misdaad in de Middeleeuwen*, 49, does mention an 'army of exiles' outside the city of Utrecht. According to him, many of the robbers sentenced in Utrecht were exiled inhabitants of Utrecht. See also Berents, *Het werk van de vos*, 80, where he mentions that some towns did not allow exiles from other places to remain in the city after dark (which suggests it was known who they were), forcing exiles into a life of vagabondage and robbery. Unfortunately, he does not supply any references for this claim.

[172] Schuster, *Stadt vor Gericht*, 248–9.

[173] Coy, 'Beggars at the gates', 620, 628.

[174] Boomgaard, *Misdaad en Straf in Amsterdam*, 156.

the century on the presence of undesirables, or basically anyone 'foreign', in the town, especially at night, but this may have been the result of concerns of morality more than economics. None of these laws were, however, specifically aimed at solving any problems with outcasts just beyond the town.[175] Perhaps the numbers being banished from Kampen were not large enough at this time to create such problems. It may also be that exiles had sufficient other places to go to in the vicinity, such as, among others, Zwolle, Elburg, Hattem and Hasselt.

As has already been pointed out, banishment perhaps created more problems than it was meant to solve. An expulsion from an urban community could be the start of an itinerant life of crime. When people lost their livelihoods, they sometimes did not have any other choice than to scrape by through stealing and robbing. If towns did not allow exiles from other places into their communities, or severely restricted the possibilities of 'strangers', then their options were limited. This is, of course, based on the assumption that magistrates knew that these people had been banished from elsewhere. It is unlikely that town councils were informed about every single person that had been cast out from other towns, but there is some evidence that there was information exchange between towns about exiles and lawbreakers.[176] Henric die Cruijsser, who was executed in Kampen in 1483 for a number of violent crimes and theft, confessed to having been banished from Utrecht.[177] Elsewhere in Europe, neighbouring towns appear to have set up various arrangements to deal with the

[175] In 1478, 1493 and 1498 by-laws were issued regulating the stay of strangers in inns (DN, f. 29r (1478); f. 47r (1493); f. 50v (1498)). In 1483 it was laid down that strangers could not walk the streets after nine o'clock (DN f. 34r (1483)). A year later the use of disguises out in the open was proscribed (DN, f. 34r (1484)). In 1496 infamous persons, common women and others like them were disallowed buying property in the city (DN, f. 49v (1496)). In 1461, 1467 and 1492 beggars were banned from begging in churches, though they were allowed to beg in churchyards and elsewhere (DN, f. 9r (1461); f. 15v (1467); f. 45v (1492)). Overall, however, regulations in Kampen against begging were surprisingly lax. See Brand and Frankot, 'Das Kampener Stadtbuch', 48–9. In Ulm, the magistrates began 'to enforce vagrancy statutes more energetically' only in the second half of the sixteenth century. Coy, 'Beggars at the gates', 626.

[176] The detailed lists of crimes committed (and confessed to) by the offenders who were mutilated or executed, for example, suggest towns were exchanging information on these matters. The 'limping man' who was flogged and banished for crimes committed in Kampen in 1455 was known to have committed manslaughter in Emmerich before. DV, f. 16v (24 April 1455). See also the case of Hendrik Hoeymaker in Chap. 5.

[177] Reg, p. 226 (17 March 1483).

problem of exiles. In 1241, Hamburg and Lübeck agreed to exchange information about fugitives and to respect each other's sentences. This agreement was later followed by wider Hanseatic collaboration. Registers concerning banishments in various towns, such as Stralsund, include entries concerning crimes from other places.[178] Thirteenth-century Valenciennes and Saint-Quentin were also communicating about exiles, aiming to make banishments effective for a large area.[179] In the Polish kingdom and Silesia, confederations of towns existed in the middle ages, and banishments were valid in all the towns of such a confederation. Presumably, the towns corresponded with each other about who was exiled.[180] In Southern Germany and Switzerland too, towns cooperated to keep exiles out of a larger area, so they were prevented from causing problems for neighbours.[181] In Göttingen, a different solution to problems with expulsed individuals was sought: there the magistrates increasingly imposed different punishments from around 1420. This also prevented any negative consequences on the economy due to the absence of productive members of society.[182]

To conclude, it is clear that the Kampen town council in the second half of the fifteenth century increasingly preferred to protect the community from the potential dangers of allowing strangers into its midst (unless, of course, these strangers came to trade goods). At the same time, it excluded more and more people, especially women, from the town community for deviant behaviour. With these actions they were most likely responding to an increasing demand from certain groups within society who denounced their neighbours for morally offensive and disruptive behaviour, and expected the magistrates to deal with the culprits. In the last quarter of the fifteenth century, there was a clear increase in the punishment of women for such acts. At the same time, though, the magistrates do not yet appear to have used rituals to accompany the physical act of exclusion in order to communicate their commitment to maintaining a well-ordered and morally pure town. Instead, banishments were perhaps only announced publicly in a number of arenas. The general public, in the meantime, do not appear to have been particularly active in capturing exiles who had returned

[178] Zaremska, *Les bannis au Moyen Âge*, 90.
[179] Huart, 'Maintenir la paix', 7–8.
[180] Zaremska, *Les bannis au Moyen Âge*, 162–3.
[181] Maurer, 'Erzwungene Ferne', 212; Marchal, '"Von der Stadt"', 253.
[182] Boockmann, *Urfehde und ewige Gefangenschaft*, 45–8.

illegally. It may be that most people were eager to denounce their neighbours when their behaviour annoyed or offended them personally.[183] However, when an exiled individual returned to town and did not bother them specifically, they might have been happy to turn a blind eye. That the magistrates could also show mercy to those that were willing to mend their ways (and arrange to pay their fines) shall become clear in the following chapter.

[183] See also Smail, *The Consumption of Justice*, 18.

CHAPTER 5

# Redemption: The Repayment of Fines and the Reintegration of Exiles

**Abstract** The second of two main chapters, this analyses the redemption of exiles and what this can tell us about the values of late medieval Kampen society concerning morally acceptable behaviour. The first section concerns the practical aspects around the reintegration of banished individuals from all categories, whereas the second section focuses specifically on the financial arrangements between exiles and magistrates which allowed the former to return to Kampen. The final section discusses the links between debt and morality, in order to establish whether defaulting public debtors were banished because they were considered to have displayed immoral behaviour.

**Keywords** Redemption • Debt • Morality • Crime

In Kampen, as in Ulm, there must have been banished offenders who did not stray too far from the town, as they either still had property there, a family, a business with customers that needed to be tended to, or a steady position. These people would have tried, most likely generally with assistance from people inside Kampen, to gather money to be able to pay off their fines or debts, or to negotiate terms with the town representatives.



E. Frankot, *Banishment in the Late Medieval Eastern Netherlands*,
https://doi.org/10.1007/978-3-030-88867-1_5

For those in debt,[1] to be allowed back was relatively straightforward: the fines or debts needed to be paid off. For those banished as a punishment, the situation was potentially more fluid, especially for those sentenced to an exile of undetermined duration. Those banished for life or for an extensive period (five or ten years) would most likely have moved away to try their luck elsewhere. For others, though, it would have been worthwhile not to stray too far from Kampen to try and negotiate a return. As mentioned above, some were banished until their conduct improved, or until they were invited to return. This chapter looks in more detail at the processes of reintegration for both groups of exiles, with a specific focus on the financial arrangements made for the payment of fines.

## Returning to the Fold

A few cases offer some information concerning the redemption of exiles after banishment as a punishment and their return to town. Dirk Witte was banished on 1 July 1473 at a distance of four miles after he had spoken badly about 'lords, princes, ladies and young women' and had been caught pairing off men and women for illegal sexual acts. He swore an *oervede* oath that he would stay at least four miles from Kampen until 'he [was] informed otherwise' ('men hem anders weten laat'). On 10 May 1474 he was allowed to return to town on condition that he would behave himself from now on, on pain of eternal banishment at a distance of six miles.[2] Goiken Henricsz was banished in 1476 for various acts of misbehaviour, for which he was imprisoned first. He swore an oath to remain at a distance of at least ten miles from Kampen on pain of losing his hand. An added note indicates that Goiken was a mariner. It says that in case he came within the ten-mile radius as a result of bad weather at sea, he should attempt to leave again as soon as possible. Goiken was allowed to return to Kampen in December 1478, so at least two years later, on condition that he stop his misbehaviour.[3] So these two men were allowed to return to the fold after having spent a significant amount of time outside the

[1] The word 'debt' (singular) as in 'to owe a debt' or 'to be in debt' is here also used to indicate the money owed to the town as a result of the non-payment of fines (as is 'debtor' as someone owing that money), in addition to the more usual meaning of 'debts' as money owed as a result of any kind of exchange (including rents) or of a loan. The word 'debts' (plural) is here only used to indicate the latter.

[2] DV, f. 125r (1 Jul 1473); Reg, p. 12 (1473); LC, f. 1v (10 May 1474).

[3] Reg, p. 14 (1476); LC, f. 8v (December 1478).

town, and on condition that they refrain in the future from the behaviour which got them in trouble in the first place. Dirk Witte is likely the same as the man by the same name that became a citizen in 1467.[4] He also appears regularly as a creditor and as a legal representative of others in the sources of the late 1470s and early 1480s, so he seems to have been a man of some financial means. Nonetheless, his offences had been considered so severe that he had been banished at a distance of four miles and had not been allowed back for more than ten months. After his return, however, he appears to have become a full member of Kampen society again, lending out money and being asked to act on other people's behalf.[5] There is no evidence that his status or reputation was affected by his crime or his banishment. Witte redeemed himself through his banishment.

Goiken Henricsz was a mariner, a profession which required men to be away from home for extensive amounts of time. In addition, it was a profession that could be undertaken from any port. This would most likely have made a banishment from one of these ports easier to bear. It seems unlikely that being banished affected Goiken's chances of finding work, and the Kampen magistrates apparently agreed, considering it likely that he might end up near the town on a ship in need, as they specifically allowed for this possibility. The fact that Goiken was allowed back more than two years later suggests that he had some connections in Kampen which made it worthwhile for him to go through the effort of a court procedure. Unfortunately, none of these cases specify how the magistrates tracked down the exiles or communicated with them. In some cases, as is also suggested by a single entry in 1462, messengers were sent out, who may have acquired information from family or friends with regard to where the outcast might be found.[6] In other cases, the procedure will have been initiated by the exile seeking to return.

Even better recorded is the case of Dirk Sandersz and Suetken, who are also portrayed next to one of the entries in the *Digestum Vetus* (see Fig. 5.1). Dirk appears to have had dark hair and a beard, whereas Suetken is shown holding up her hand (like Hille in Fig. 4.3?), though it is unclear what this gesture might indicate. In September 1459 they were found guilty of double adultery, meaning that both parties were married to

[4] BB, f. 134v (1467).

[5] SR, f. 31r (1475); LT, f. 114v (1485); SAK, RA, no. 75, f. 47v (4 November 1476) and f. 57r (9 June 1477).

[6] Reg, p. 6: 'eeir men hem baden sendt'.

**Fig. 5.1** Suetken and Diric Sandersz (DV, f. 34r (27 September 1459)). (© Stadsarchief Kampen, Nederland/© City Archives Kampen, the Netherlands)

another person when they committed adultery. They were sentenced to banishment. Only four weeks later, on 25 October, Dirk had been readmitted and was back in court, where he promised not to have any more to do with Suetken. He also vouched to live peacefully with his wife Hille and to share his meals and his bed with her as a good husband should ('mit Hillen synen echten wyve restlich ende vredelic leven sal ende mit haer to mete ende to male gaen, ende to bedde als een guet man mit sijnen wijve schuldich is toe gaene').[7] On 13 November of the same year a note was added to this entry that Suetken had been readmitted too, under the same conditions.

The story does not end there. In 1467 Dirk Sandersz was banished again, at a distance of one mile, as is evident from an oath in the *oerveden*

[7] DV, f. 34r (27 September 1459); f. 34r (25 October 1459). In 1457 Dirk had already been in court for insulting the market master. DV, f. 26r (7 April 1457).

register, though it is unclear why.[8] At the start of 1468 Dirk was back in court, perhaps returning from his banishment. This time he was told that he would not be allowed to farm any of the town's fishing rights or conduct any trade on the fish market, but only directly from his house. He was told again to act like a husband to his wife Hille. In addition, he was disallowed to go into the courthouse, except on business, and would no longer be allowed to act as a witness. The reason for all this was that he had broken his oath, possibly that made in 1459 on his return to Kampen. Any future misbehaviour would result in lifelong banishment.[9]

In 1473, finally, Suetken (by then a widow) was back in court, having been readmitted after another banishment. The reason for the banishment had been that Dirk Sandersz had been found in her house. This time she was warned that if they would be caught again, she would be declared forfeit of all her goods within the freedom of Kampen.[10] There is no mention of a sentence for Dirk in the *Digestum Vetus*, but there is another oath in the *oerveden* register from that same year in which he promised to stay away from Kampen at a distance of four miles.[11] There is no mention whether this banishment was meant to be permanent, in accordance with the 1468 warning. From his appearance in other sources from December 1474 onwards, it appears that he was not permanently banished. In 1478, his wife Hille was named as his widow, so he must have died in 1477 or 1478. Judging by the sources, Dirk Sandersz was likely a man of some financial means and standing, possibly a fish merchant, and a citizen.[12] As such, the magistrates would probably have preferred not to exclude him permanently from their midst despite his regular perceived immoral behaviour. Nonetheless, they gave out a clear message that such behaviour was not acceptable by banishing Dirk at least three times. Unfortunately, we do not know how long the second and third banishments were and whether they got increasingly longer, for example. It is notable that Dirk's first banishment was shorter than that of his female partner. By allowing Dirk (and Suetken) back into the fold on a number of occasions, the magistrates could display their mercy and their willingness to reintegrate those

[8] Reg, p. 9 (1467).

[9] DV, f. 77$^{bis}$v (30 January 1468).

[10] DV, f. 130r (28 September 1473).

[11] Reg, p. 12 (1473).

[12] There does not appear to be a record of a Dirk Sandersz in the 'burgerboek'. He appears as a creditor in a number of documents, as does Hille, for example in SAK, RA, no. 75, f. 17r (2 December 1474). Hille appears as Dirk's widow in SAK, RA, no. 76, f. 34v (14 May 1478).

who chose to better their lives. It is likely that the magistrates expected humility and contrition on the part of the former exiles, though there is no evidence of any rituals of reintegration. The magistrates did, at least temporarily, take away some of Dirk Sandersz's rights, but this was a result of him breaking his oath, rather than of the adultery itself, or of the banishment. And despite this, Dirk continued to be able to trade.

Looking back on the case of Suetken and Dirk today it may appear sad that their (love) affair, which lasted for at least 15 years, had such grave repercussions on their lives. Of course, we also should take into account the possibility that Dirk stalked and sexually harassed Suetken for more than 15 years.[13] The Kampen magistrates in the fifteenth century were especially concerned with keeping the peace. Long-term extra-marital affairs could potentially cause a breach of the peace or other problems, such as those related to the existence of any illegal offspring and inheritances. In the second half of the fifteenth century the question of immorality also increasingly became a factor when judging such affairs. This was influenced by the already mentioned preaching of Observant friars like Brugman and by an increase of denunciations for adultery.[14] As was elaborated upon in the previous chapter, this focus appears to have become more pronounced in the final quarter of the fifteenth century. This change is also reflected in the language that the magistrates used.

Other clues with regard to the return of outcasts can be found in the banishment register itself. As we know, this register mainly concerns banishment for debt (including the non-payment of fines), rather than banishment as a punishment. Of 1267 people recorded there between 1447 and 1500, 410 entries (32.4 per cent) were crossed out, meaning that the entries were no longer valid. Though occasionally evidence points to other reasons for entries becoming obsolete, the vast majority of them were

[13] I am grateful to Christine Ekholst and other contributors to the 'Confronting Sexual Violence' roundtable at the International Medieval Congress in Leeds in 2019 for pointing out that we should not necessarily take the legal terminology of sexual crimes in court records at face value. What is termed 'fornication' (or 'adultery' for that matter) may have been rape in actual fact.

[14] Brand and Frankot, 'Das Kampener Stadtbuch', 53; Carlier, *Kinderen van der minne?*, 106–110; Carlier and Stabel, 'Questions de moralité', 256, 258–60. For a similar development in Italy under influence of friars like Bernardino, see Dean, *Crime and Justice in Late Medieval Italy*, 138, 154. Concerning aspects of property and adultery, see also Crawford, *European Sexualities*, 148–50.

most likely deleted because the debt was paid off.[15] We know for certain that they were paid with regard to about a third of entries that were deleted since 1465 (105 out of 316 people between 1465–1500) as their protagonists appear in the *jaarkeur* register as having arranged a repayment scheme with the town magistrates. We will focus on this group in more detail in the next section.

Although it is evident that Kampen's administration was not faultless (a number of entries were left undeleted despite the exiles appearing in the *jaarkeur* register settling their debt), it is likely that the majority of the remaining two-thirds of 1276 outcasts did not return from their banishment.[16] One is said to have died.[17] This could be because they were unable or unwilling to pay off their fines in order to be allowed to re-join the Kampen community.[18] It is also possible that some were not given an opportunity by the town council to redeem themselves. As was clear from the *oerveden* register, a few of the individuals who were ousted following some time in custody for the non-payment of their fine were banished from Kampen permanently (see Chap. 4). It is likely that many of these groups of exiles had no close connections to the town and were itinerant workmen (or women), some of whom may have been cast out of other communities. Instead of troubling themselves with settling large fines in order to return to a place where they would never receive full citizenship privileges, if they were even allowed this, they are likely to have tried to start anew in another town. Others would have turned (or returned) to a life on the road. The sharing of information between towns (see Chap. 4) might, of course, have restricted options somewhat.

The worst cases of such itinerant outcasts can be found in the *Digestum Vetus* and the register of capital and corporal punishment. There we find long confessions, detailing thefts, robberies and murders conducted in

[15] For example, Jorgen Rijnscher, banished in 1475 following his flight after having committed some acts of violence, was flogged in 1478, which appears to have been considered sufficient to pay off his fine after a three-year banishment (Reg, p. 124); Coert Keest, Herman Wachter, Aernt Coster and Dirk Blome 'carried candles' in 1492 to make amends for the illegal chopping of wood (Reg, p. 142); in 1464 Mijnte carried the stone for a fine of 180 lb., a highly unusual display of mercy by the town magistrates (Reg, p. 103).

[16] The relevant counterparts of 12 of 105 entries of the *jaarkeur* have not been deleted in the banishment register. The administration appears to have gotten more accurate in the second half of the period (see also below): ten entries are from the 1465–1482 period, only two from the 1483–1500 period.

[17] Reg, p. 120 (1474).

[18] Cf. Zaremska, *Les bannis au Moyen Âge*, 160.

various regions of the Low Countries, northern France and western Germany. These confessions, as mentioned before most likely admitted to under duress (though they had to be confirmed in court to become valid as evidence),[19] were all made by visitors to Kampen. The confessors were generally executed. The already mentioned Hendrik die Cruyser, for example, confessed to having been banished from Utrecht, wounding a man in Deventer who subsequently died, as well as committing other woundings, possibly in Kampen as that is where he was eventually beheaded in 1483.[20] Hans Oesterling confessed to several thefts, many conducted with others, in a large area covering much of the Netherlands and the north-east of Germany: Groningen, Friesland, Harderwijk, Utrecht, Purmerend, Haarlem, Leiden, Den Haag, Scheveningen, Delft, Gouda, Dordrecht, Brouwershaven, Arnemuiden, Middelburg, Vlissingen, Sluis, Bremen, Stade and other places, including Kampen where he tried to steal a wooden statue from St Nicholas church. He was beheaded, perhaps symbolically, on Saint Nicholas' Eve 1469.[21] It is such cases that highlight the potentially very negative consequences of a banishment for both individuals and the urban community, and the difficulty some individuals had in redeeming themselves.

Of many men and women, we do not know where they ended up, as looking for them would mean searching through the sources of many Dutch, German and Belgian towns in case they ended up in court elsewhere. Occasionally there is a chance encounter with a former Kampen inhabitant: in Leiden in 1494 Hendrik Hoeymaker was arrested. It was known that he had been banished (probably in absentia) from Kampen after a manslaughter. He was eventually allowed to stay in Leiden after a large payment was made which may have been used to settle the case with the victim's family or to settle the fine with the Kampen authorities.[22] It may well be that this payment would also have allowed him to return to Kampen. The fact that the Leiden authorities knew of the Kampen manslaughter, and that the Kampen magistrates had details of many crimes

[19] For example, in 1493 Geert van Walsem in court retracted his confession that he murdered four merchants with three other men. He was still drawn and broken on the wheel for several thefts and robberies with murder. Reg, p. 235 (10 Jun 1493).

[20] Reg, p. 226 (17 March 1483).

[21] DV, f. 95r (5 December 1469).

[22] Glaudemans, *Om die wrake wille*, 202. Glaudemans does not mention the possibility that the money may have been used for settling the fine. I have as yet been unable to locate this manslaughter in the Kampen sources.

committed elsewhere as evidenced in the confessions by those sentenced to death, confirms that a lively correspondence was conducted between the towns in the Netherlands and its bordering regions.[23] The case also suggests that individuals were able to find a home elsewhere after a banishment, especially when they had professions sought after in a particular town.

As it is difficult to gain a complete picture of the social circumstances of the offenders who were banished, it is also hard to get a clear profile of the people who were able to return to Kampen compared to those who were not. It is likely that among the former group were more outcasts who had citizenship, more who owned property or a business, and more who had a family and a social network in Kampen. As will become clear in the following section, a network of people who could stand surety for the payments that a reintegrating outcast had to pay was vital to be able to set up a financial arrangement with the town. In that respect it is perhaps surprising to note that relatively few offenders for whom a profession is recorded in the banishment register arranged to pay their fine in instalments. The vast majority (127 out of 149 for whom we know a profession) appears to have left Kampen for good. For example, of 19 fullers registered as banished, only 1 appears to have returned, of 15 weavers only 3, and of 10 tailors also just 3. The textile producing business appears to have been one with a high turnover of staff, presumably employing relatively many newcomers to the town. The same turnover can be recognised among the millers, where only one out of ten returned (and one died), and smiths of whom none came back of nine who were banished.

A possible reason for the relatively high percentage of offenders with a named profession who did not seek to come back to town is that relatively many people who did not originate in Kampen were identified by additional characteristics such as their profession or their place of origin. It may be that others who appeared in the sources did not need any further identification because they were known inhabitants of Kampen. Though Kampen was a reasonably sizeable town by medieval standards, it is likely that most people knew each other in a population of about 6000–8500. And, as has already been argued, people without strong links to the town were more likely to try out their luck elsewhere after banishment. It is

[23] Concerning correspondence about criminal activities, see also Coy, *Strangers and Misfits*, 11; Vanhemelryck, *Misdadigers tussen recht en beul*, 26; Zaremska, *Les bannis au Moyen Âge*, 90–91, 163.

likely that men with professions like textile workers, tailors, smiths and millers would have had no trouble finding work elsewhere (assuming their status as an exile did not interfere with this). That offenders without strong links to Kampen were less likely to return is also suggested by the fact that not one of the exiles who were identified by a geographical name sought reintegration.

Nonetheless, Kampen, like most medieval towns, was a place inhabited by many newcomers. The extant register of citizens, which unfortunately ends in 1469, includes many men, and some women, who gained citizenship after having migrated to Kampen from other places in the Low Countries and neighbouring German regions. An analysis of the register for the 50 years from 1420 to 1469 suggests that it does not include the sons of already existing citizens. None of the established Kampen families who supplied councillors and aldermen appear in the register, for example. These sons perhaps became citizens automatically or their registration was seriously flawed.[24] Others had to pay to become burghers, and a by-law of 1485 laid down (or perhaps confirmed an already existing rule) that the children of the people who applied to become citizens also became citizens (on payment of a fee, of course). If the parents did not want this, none of them would be allowed to gain citizenship.[25] It is noteworthy that the by-law speaks of 'olders' (parents), not just of the father. Women could and did on occasion become burghers and there are examples of mothers with sons (or daughters) becoming citizens. On the other hand, at least up until 1469, it was normally only the sons of the family who were registered in the *Burgerboek* with their fathers, so we should perhaps not read too much into the gender-unspecific terminology used in this by-law.

In the 50 years from 1420 to 1469, 2608 new citizens were registered, approximately 52 per annum. In some years, such as 1445 and 1453 close to a hundred new burghers were accepted. This does not generally include the wives or daughters who, no doubt, had also come along to live in Kampen, nor those who did not pay for citizenship. Of these 2608 people, 66 or 67 were women, so just over one per year. Occasionally these were widows, presumably of deceased burghers, but others were clearly

[24] Prak (*Citizens without nations*, 34) confirms that the registration of born citizens elsewhere was also incomplete and that they appear to have often taken their citizenship for granted.

[25] DN, f. 35v (1485).

migrants, such as Balyaene Hermansdochter of Quadebrede and Herman Swane, her son.[26]

As was suggested in Chap. 2, there do not appear to have been any restrictions in place on becoming a citizen in Kampen. Not many of the names are accompanied by a profession, but those that are (103 of them) include a variety of craftsmen. Strangely, in 1468, eight millers were accepted in a single year.[27] Those that include a placename (303 entries) also show a wide geographical spread, from some of the larger towns in the bordering German lands, such as Bremen, Münster and Osnabrück, to those in the Low Countries (Groningen, Amersfoort, Utrecht, Dordrecht, Zierikzee and Den Bosch, for example) to towns and villages closer by. Many came with children: 410 were fathers (or mothers) with at least one son (or daughter) registered at the same time. Some were very large families indeed: nine men had five sons each and two had six. Johan Wolff, who gained citizenship in 1425, even brought along nine sons: Wolf, Arnt, Evert, Wyllem, Esken, Cracht, Alfer, another Wyllem and Johan.[28]

It is unclear whether there were any residence requirements prior to a person becoming a citizen.[29] A 1559 ordinance suggests that it might have been possible to acquire citizenship on arrival, as long as a person could submit evidence of good reputation, the proper Christian religion ('van gueden Christlicken geloven ende doechdeliken erberen leven ende sonder quade fame van enige moetwillige feijten offte heresien sijn') and no history of manslaughter. The ordinance had been issued because, apparently, 'many strange, foreign and unknown' ('vrembde, uutheimische ende unbecande') people were thronging to Kampen wanting to buy citizenship and make use of the common pasture lands. New citizens needed to realise, however, that there was a requirement to actually live in the town.[30] It is likely that if migrants could buy citizenship on arrival at this time,

[26] BB, f. 104r (1423).

[27] As there is no specific evidence of many millers having been banished in previous years, this may have had something to do with the extension of the town which had started around 1462.

[28] BB, f. 105r.

[29] The answer to this can probably be found in F.C. Berkenvelder, *Stedelijk burgerrecht en burgerschap. Een verkennende inventarisatie in Deventer, Kampen en Zwolle (1302–1811)* (Zwolle 2005), but I came across this title too late to be able to access it for this publication.

[30] 'Die vrije ordinantie … vanden ingecofften burgers ende die in burgers gemoede sitten' (21 February 1559), in: *Overijsselsche Stad-, Dijk- en Markeregten*, 237–41, specifically 238.

when the magistrates were obviously concerned about the number of aliens knocking on the town gates and about their religion, they would most likely also have been able to do this in the second half of the fifteenth century. That does not mean that all migrants immediately became citizens. It is likely that most lived in the town for a while to establish themselves before applying for citizenship.

This openness to migrants able to pay for citizenship rights suggests that the town was doing fine economically and could use additional productive members of society. This was no doubt also to fill up gaps left as a result of a high urban mortality rate and an average 26–27 banishments per year, of which only about a third returned, as we have seen. One of the downsides of banishment was, of course, that it might rid the town of useful people. Citizenship does not seem to have been restricted to a small group, and many craftsmen were citizens, as were some members in the service industry, such as porters. The porters had their own guild and, according to a 1500 by-law, the town magistrates allowed that only two out of three guild masters needed to be burghers because not so many of them were.[31] That the porters were relatively well-respected members of society is also clear from the fact that a number of them appear as guarantors for the people arranging to pay their fine in instalments.[32]

All of this suggests that the town magistrates were not principally against, or suspicious of, outsiders. Quite the contrary: there was a healthy influx of newcomers every year. Over 50 new (mostly male) citizens were accepted every year, most likely bringing along another 50 female family members on average. Of course, some of these new citizens would have already been living in Kampen. Moreover, there were those who could not afford to become citizens, but were attracted by job opportunities. In addition, the town was frequented by merchants and skippers from elsewhere.

Another hint that the magistrates did not seek to restrict access to the Kampen community to productive members of society is the fact that they facilitated offenders redeeming themselves by arranging financial terms. Again, the social circumstances of those seeking reintegration in this way are not easy to establish. Of the ones whose profession is mentioned in the

[31] DN, f. 51v.

[32] For example, Albert Jansz who appears a couple of times as a guarantor. Reg, p. 407 (1493), p. 410 (1494).

banishment register, a variety of craftsmen are included, as well as two servants, a fisherman, a parson and a head boatswain. It is likely that the same variety existed among those whose professions we do not know. In the *jaarkeur* register, a similarly varied group can be found, though again the numbers are small: the profession of only 26 of the debtors who had been banished before they arranged to pay their fine is known. It is perhaps noteworthy that 9 of these 26 were Rhine skippers, but the share of Rhine skippers in this register is relatively high anyway: of 68 professions of debtors named in total, 12 were Rhine skippers, and 30 of 135 guarantors were too. No other profession comes close to being as prominent in this register as this group of men who were relatively prone to violence, but who also had a guild, an extensive network and some wealth and social standing.

There does not appear to be a marked difference between the varied social status of the people who arranged for the payment of their fine immediately and those who did so after a banishment. Both groups include servants, a variety of craftsmen and skippers. The only group that may be lacking is that of the wealthiest citizens who had probably been able to pay a fine outright. But a sample analysis of the lists of fines and other sources from 1490 shows that there were very few who could afford to pay the highest fines immediately. Of 156 fines which appear to have been paid immediately, the majority were smaller fines of 20 s. (21 fines), 100 s. (17 fines) and 2 (*hern*?) lb. (64 fines).[33] Of the fines for woundings, only two were paid outright: one of 100 lb. and one of 200 lb.[34] The others, at least 19 including 2 homicides, ended up arranging the payment of their fines in instalments or they were banished.[35] There was also one person who arranged to pay his fine of 200 lb. for adultery in instalments.[36] The difference between offenders who immediately arranged for the payment of a fine, and those who did not and ended up having to negotiate their return to the city after they had probably mostly fled the town, was probably small. The difference may mainly have been one of the circumstances of the offence and its aftermath. But, as previously noted, we know very little about the sequence of events that led to so many becoming outcasts after

[33] LT, ff. 143r-144r, 160r-161v, 163r; SR, ff. 181v-183v.

[34] SR, f. 182r (Claes Allertsz 25 *hern* lb.); LT, f. 143r (Johan Glynchagen 50 *hern* lb.).

[35] Not all the entries in the lists of fines that indicate a banishment specify an offence, and some cannot be found in any of the other sources.

[36] LT, f. 143r and SR, f. 182r.

fineable offences. We know more about what happened when such outcasts were able to negotiate their return, which is the subject of the next section.

## Financial Arrangements Between Town and Exiles

About a third of the men and women who ended up as outcasts because of unpaid fines or debts did come back to Kampen after they had arranged for a payment in terms with the magistrates. From at least 1465, these financial arrangements were recorded in the *jaarkeur* register. Between 1465 and 1500, the register concerns 281 persons. Of these, 104 can also be found in the register of banishments. The rest likely arranged for payment of their fines on conviction, rather than being banished for failure to pay (or fleeing before their trial). These offenders had perhaps been better able to secure sureties from family members and friends or perhaps had a better reputation among the magistrates, and they had not panicked on having committed their offences. For example, in 1486 Andries Vierholt was fined 50 *hern* lb. for wounding someone at night. It was arranged that he would pay his fine in five terms, the first one in 1486. Seven men stood surety for him.[37] Vierholt was a man of some means who also rented town properties, for some of which he had to pay more than 50 *hern* lb. annually.[38] But there were also people of lower social status, such as Geertken Jansdochter, a maidservant who managed to pay off a 20 *hern* lb. fine in just two instalments. The register details that she had already paid the first. It would have been likely that her employers stepped in to assist her, but she only had one person standing surety for her, and it was not her boss.[39] So it is unclear how this woman managed to bring together this significant sum of money in such a short period.

Nearly two-thirds of the outcasts who negotiated a financial arrangement with the magistrates did so in the year in which they had been banished, and 25 did in the following calendar year. Few of the entries in the banishment register are dated precisely, so it is not possible to determine the exact times that people spend outwith the town. Only in 11 cases did exiles take longer in trying to negotiate a return. Most likely these people

[37] Reg, p. 391 (October or November 1486); LT, f. 115v (1486).

[38] For example, SR, f. 173v (1490): one rental of 28½ lb. 25 pl. paid in one term, and one of 67 lb. 18 pl. paid in two terms.

[39] Reg, p. 404.

tried their luck elsewhere first, or actually moved somewhere else, before deciding that they wanted or needed to return after all. Two offenders returned about two years after their banishment, four exiles three years later and one each four and five years after having left. There are three outcasts who appear not to have come back for a long time, though we should take into account the possibility that a first return and second exile are missing from the records. On the other hand, the fines in these three cases add up. In 1478 Henric Palmer arranged to pay for a 100 lb. fine, a fine that appears to date back to 1465.[40] Even more extreme are the cases of Hessel Petersz and Herman Schuefstake who returned after about 22 and 23 years respectively. Schuefstake's fines, 100 lb. for a wounding plus 2 lb., add up exactly to those he was banished for in 1467. Petersz was banished for a 100 lb. fine in 1463 and paid off 25 *hern* lb. in 1485.[41]

But, as said, mostly offenders negotiated their return to Kampen within a year of their banishment (or flight) and most likely within a few weeks or months, as there was likely no other impediment to their return beyond the payment of the fine. On the other hand, seeing that the magistrates offered the possibility to arrange to pay off fines in instalments, there must have been other factors in play when an offender chose to flee. Most likely this was to escape any potential wrath from the victim and/or his or her relatives. Also, in cases of wounding, an offender may not necessarily have known whether or not his victim survived or would survive, and in cases of manslaughter a reconciliation usually needed to take place before a culprit could be welcomed back into the community.[42] Finally, offenders may have been worried about being subject to a flogging, like a few of the individuals recorded in the *oerveden* register were (see Chap. 4).

As soon as a financial arrangement was agreed upon with an exile, the entry in the register of banishments was deleted. The deletion did not depend upon the full payment of the fine. This was similar to the practice in the Prussian towns of Kulm and Thorn where the entry concerning an exile was deleted within eight days of the agreed return to town, though

[40] Reg, p. 382 (12 July 1478).

[41] Petersz: Reg, p. 102 (1463), p. 358 (9 July 1485); Schuefstake: Reg, p. 108 (1467), Reg, p. 404 (December 1490).

[42] At least, according to the 1385 by-law. BvR, f. 22v (1385). The 1426 by-law does not specify whether a reconciliation was still required in addition to the 400 lb. fine. GB, f. 48r (1426). See also Chap. 4.

there this was usually after a compensation payment was made in full.[43] In Kampen, most of the payments were ultimately paid in full, after which the entry in the *jaarkeur* register was also deleted. There are a few examples of cases in which the full amount due was not paid. These entries remained undeleted in the *jaarkeur* register, but the relevant entries in the banishment register were crossed out. For example, Jan Tymansz was deemed a fugitive and exile after he had wounded a man on a ship during daytime in 1495.[44] This crime was subject to a fine of 100 lb./25 *hern* lb. In 1496 Tymansz arranged to pay off his debt in eight instalments: 4 *hern* lb. to be paid during the reign of the current aldermen, and then 3 *hern* lb. every year until the fine was paid in full (the final term was in 1503). The notes on payments in the margins reveal that Tymansz paid his first six terms, but not the last two.[45] It is not clear why not. Perhaps he died or moved elsewhere. In 1487 Johan Starke was due a fine of 25 *hern* lb., 10 of which he paid in cash straight away (perhaps on his return to Kampen). The rest would be paid in five terms of 3 lb. Starke never paid these terms and the *jaarkeur* states that he died.[46] He did not die straight away, though, as the annual *jaarkeur* lists in the town accounts from 1492, 1493 and 1494 noted that he was still due the remainder of several terms, and had sworn an oath to pay these.[47] Unfortunately, the account does not go beyond 1494, so that we do not have an exact year of his death. Up until 1494 Starke was perhaps urged to pay, but may have been unable. No measures to evict him from the town appear to have been undertaken.

Another case of non-payment sheds some light on the procedure of arranging readmission into the town community. Stijne Tade had appeared in court twice in 1484. At the end of August, she was forbidden to draw any more beer, on punishment of 40 lb.[48] Between 9 and 15 September she was back in court, but this time on much heavier charges: facilitating illegal sexual acts ('quade herberg'), keeping bad company at night and by day and generally leading an immoral life. As a punishment she was made to stay away from the town at a distance of at least one mile, on punish-

[43] In these towns, the punishment for a wounding was the cutting off of the hand (as it had been in Kampen originally for a wounding at night), but this could usually be compensated, hence the need to pay a compensation in full. Jeziorski, 'Die Strafe der Ausweisung', 37–9.

[44] Reg, p. 145 (1495).

[45] Reg, p. 409 (1496).

[46] Reg, p. 393 (9 June 1487).

[47] SR, f. 205v (1492); f. 219v (1493); f. 234v (1494).

[48] LC, f. 16r (31 August 1484).

ment of the 'kaak'.[49] Judging by the *oerveden* register, Tade returned unauthorised later that year. She was put in prison and on the 'kaak', and was now made to swear to stay at least ten miles from the town, on punishment of losing an ear.[50]

Six years later, in 1490, her name appears in the *jaarkeur* register. Three men stood surety for her and promised that she would pay the town 20 *hern* lb. in two terms.[51] The first instalment would be paid 'wanneer sie ynkompt' ('when she enters [Kampen]'), the second a year later. But it appears that she decided against coming back, as a note was added later, stating 'sie is toch niet inkomen' ('she has not returned after all').[52] There are also entries in the *jaarkeur* lists in the town accounts of 1491, 1492 and 1493 (but not in 1494), obviously keeping open the option of her return for a few years after her representatives had renegotiated it.[53] In this case, then, the exile did not arrange her own return, but it was arranged on her behalf by three middlemen. Why she decided not to return to the city after all remains unknown. Perhaps 20 *hern* lb. was too much for her in the end.

This is not the only case in which it is specifically mentioned that others stood surety for a debt of an exile who had apparently not yet returned to arrange a repayment plan themselves. In the very first entry in the register, it is noted that Henric Aerntsz would pay his first term between now and 'sijnre incompst': his entry.[54] In 1490, too, a debtor made his first payment 'doe hie yn quam': when he entered.[55] In 1491 a mother helped arrange the return of her daughter by promising the guarantor her daughter's hooded cloak as security 'als sie ynde stad komet': when she enters the town.[56] Such pieces of evidence are, however, scarce. In most cases it is stated that the first term needed to be paid before a certain date, and there is no mention of this first payment being a condition for the return. In most cases it was the debtor themselves who was named first in the

[49] LC, f. 16v (in September (between 9 and 15) 1484).

[50] Reg, p. 19 (1484).

[51] It is possible that Taede returned to Kampen before 1490 and subsequently incurred a 20 *hern* lb. fine, as this is otherwise the only case on record where an exile pays to return after a banishment punishment.

[52] Reg, p. 403 (1 July 1490).

[53] SR, f. 192v (1491), f. 205v (1492) and f. 219v (1493).

[54] Reg, p. 372 (25 December 1465).

[55] Reg, p. 403 (25 September 1490).

[56] Reg, p. 405 (1491, after 15 July).

entry. This suggests that they negotiated with the magistrates directly, though initial mediation by others may have taken place before, seeing that exiles were not allowed to enter the city and they may not all have had the means or ability to write a letter.[57]

That the role of others was quite important in restoring a person to the town community is suggested by the lay-out of most of the first few entries in the register. In those the pledges are mentioned first and appear as the main actors in the agreements reached. The three guarantors for Henric van Leyden, for example, promised together and each for all that Henric's 20 *hern* lb. debt would be paid in five terms.[58] After the first few entries, the lay-out changes and from then on, the entries usually mention the debtor first. It is likely that pledges played a similarly deciding role in many of the other cases, even although this is not specifically mentioned. For one, guarantors were necessary to ensure payment. The debtors in question had displayed behaviour, that is to say they failed to pay or fled the town to avoid payment or even appearing in court, that made them untrustworthy and unreliable partners from the point of view of the town council. The debtor's social network was therefore a deciding factor in the magistrates' decision to allow someone to return and to trust that the debt would be paid. This confirms that the functioning of law and justice depended on cooperation and consensus within a set of complex social relations between magistrates, offenders and their networks.[59] In Kampen there is evidence that the pledges at times paid off part of the debt. By standing surety, they put their reputation on the line.[60] There are a number of examples in which the debtors promised to keep the pledges 'schadeloos', that is to say not to subject them to pecuniary liability, by putting up their property as security. These entries also confirm that at least some of the exiles had not only a social network, which made them eager to return to Kampen, but also property. The already mentioned Henric Aerntsz, for example, set his house, garden, horses and cows as security. A wagoner offered all his good horses and his wagon.[61]

[57] Maurer ('Erzwungene Ferne', 214) also notes that the records show that others put in requests for the return of exiles.

[58] Reg, p. 372 (1465).

[59] Blauert, *Das Urfehdewesen*, 68–9.

[60] It is not clear why the guarantors were not made to pay the remainder of the fines in the cases mentioned above.

[61] Reg, p. 410 (November 1494).

Standing surety were often family members (mostly fathers and brothers), masters or fellow tradesmen. There are few women, but that is not unexpected.[62] More often women (usually wives, but also mothers) promised to keep the pledges harmless by putting up collateral.[63] In the case of Henric Aerntsz, two of his brothers stood surety for him, in addition to one other man. The Rhine skippers in particular appeared regularly in the *jaarkeur* records as pledges for their colleagues. A good example of this is when Herman Schuefstake, a Rhine skipper who had been banished following a wounding, needed help: five of his pledges were also Rhine skippers.[64] Four of the guarantors of Derick Geertsz, a basket maker who had committed a wounding at night, were colleagues of his.[65] In many cases, though, it is unclear what the relation between pledges and debtor was. It is likely that fellow guild members played an important role, but few guild records survive for the middle ages. A more thorough prosopographical and relational analysis may be able to throw more light on this, but falls outside the scope of this study. Schuster, too, stressed the importance of an offender's social network. In Konstanz, family members had a joint responsibility to pay fines. High fines sometimes proved too much of a burden for someone with a small or non-existent social network. The system of penalties in Konstanz, as that in Kampen, certainly favoured the rich and well-connected.[66] In medieval Venice, inmates could be let out of prison if they could provide pledges and a promise that the debt would be paid in annual instalments. This was only offered to those who were expected to have a steady income.[67] So elsewhere, too, social networks were vital to debtors and their ability to maintain part of the town community.

Some men appear as pledges on a number of occasions and in several sources. A number of them were publicans, that is to say men with a profession that brought them into contact with many people, and especially those involved in violence as a result of brawls. One of these men was Gijsbert Blanckert, who appears as a guarantor several times, both in the *jaarkeur* and in the *Liber Testium*, and over a long period (between 1466

[62] One example is Alijt Lodewich's wife, Reg, p. 374 (1466).
[63] For example, Reg, p. 377 (1482), p. 384 (1481), p. 387 (1485).
[64] Reg, p. 404 (December 1490).
[65] Reg, p. 395 (27 December 1488).
[66] Schuster, *Stadt vor Gericht*, 257, 315.
[67] Geltner, *The Medieval Prison*, 15, 60.

and 1491). He also figures as a pledge in the town accounts.[68] Another who features often is Berent Jansz, the publican of the 'Inden Witten Aern'.[69] From 1489 at the latest the town hired two 'voirspraken', defenders: Wicher (no last name given, but probably Rensinck)[70] and Geert Wissinck. They were paid 28 and 12 pounds per annum respectively.[71] Wissinck, for example, also appears regularly in the *Liber Testium* and the town account as a guarantor, though never in the *jaarkeur*.[72] It may be that, in cases of banished debtors, the magistrates required pledges who were willing to risk their reputation and who could speak from personal experience, rather than guarantors on the town's payroll.

In a few cases no guarantors were found, but the magistrates were amenable nonetheless. One of these is from 1480 and the debtor was a foreigner: Johan de Leke of Kalkar, but living in Hamburg. Though there is no mention of his crime in the entry, his fine (50 *hern* lb.) suggests that he had committed a wounding at night.[73] This is confirmed by the fact that his probable opponent, Johan Mesmaker, was banished for wounding him at night in the same year.[74] De Leke himself was apparently not banished, but arranged to pay his large fine. Instead of providing guarantors, De Leke swore an oath to pay his debt in ten instalments, an oath which was signed and sealed with his own seal, suggesting that he was a merchant. The fact that he was allowed to swear, rather than being required to find guarantors, also indicates that he was considered trustworthy, though one would think that a merchant should have had no difficulty in finding people to stand surety for him. It appears, however, that De Leke did not return to pay off his fine: the entry remains undeleted, as do those recording the annual instalments in the lists in the town accounts (see Fig. 5.2).[75]

[68] Reg, pp. 373, 378, 382, 385, 386, 394, 404; LT, ff. 2v (2x), 36r, 72r, 75r, 132r, 160r; SR, f. 182v. For more information on Blankert and his tavern as a legal space used for business transactions, see Frankot, 'Legal business outside the courts', 181–2.

[69] For example, Reg, p. 392 (1486), p. 406 (1492), p. 420 (1499).

[70] Rensinck appears regularly in the town accounts, for example eight times as a pledge in 1490: SR, ff. 182v-183v.

[71] SR, f. 167r (1489); f. 179v (1490).

[72] For example, in 1490: LT, ff. 160r (2x), 160v (2x), 161r (2x); SR, ff. 181v (1x), 182r (3x), 182v (5x), 183r (2x).

[73] Reg, p. 384 (1480).

[74] Reg, p. 128 (1480).

[75] From 1484 onwards the accounts note the payment due for that year and of those still remaining for the previous years. There are no more entries after 1490, the year in which the debt should normally have been paid off. It appears that the magistrates gave up hope that

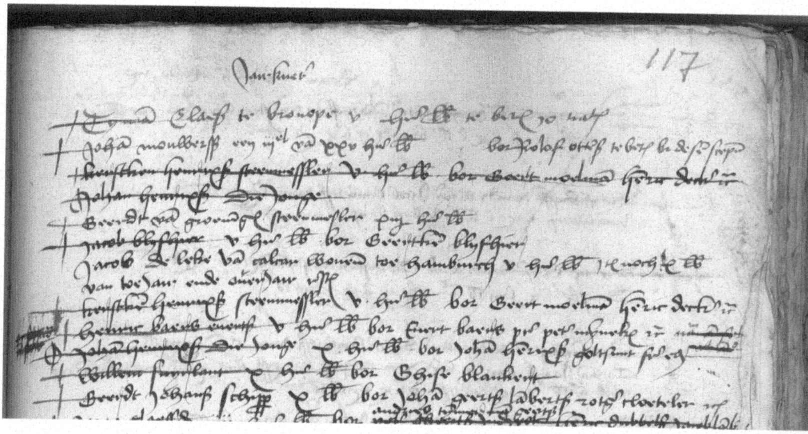

**Fig. 5.2** Detail from a page from the town accounts listing the annual *jaarkeur* payments, with Jacob die Leke's entry as the only one not deleted (SR, f. 117r (1485)). (© Stadsarchief Kampen, Nederland/© City Archives Kampen, the Netherlands)

The other three men who swore an oath also did not pay off their debt, though one of them, a man from Alkmaar living in Danzig whose case was entered in 1493, does appear to have paid once, in 1496, perhaps on his next visit to the town.[76] This does suggest that the swearing of oaths alone was not a very effective way of securing someone's cooperation, as opposed to the use of guarantors.

The Kampen magistrates adhered very strictly to the by-laws when meting out fines in the lower court. They never once, for example, deviated from the set 100 lb. (25 *hern* lb.) fine for a wounding during the day and 200 lb. (50 *hern* lb.) for a wounding at night. This is contrary to the legal practice in Konstanz where the magistrates were more flexible in meting out fines for lighter offences, but adhered strictly to the law with regard to the most serious crimes.[77] The Kampen courts were much more flexible when it came to agreeing terms for the payment of fines (as they were when passing judgement in the higher court). Presumably in such cases

De Leke would return after that date. SR, f. 83r (1481); f. 91r (1482); f. 99r (1483); f. 107r (1484); f. 117r (1485); f. 129r (1486); f. 140r (1487); f. 154r (1488); f. 168r (1489); f. 180v (1490).

[76] Reg, p. 407 (Oct 1493). The other two are on p. 386 (1484) and p. 393 (9 Jun 1487).

[77] Schuster, *Stadt vor Gericht*, 207.

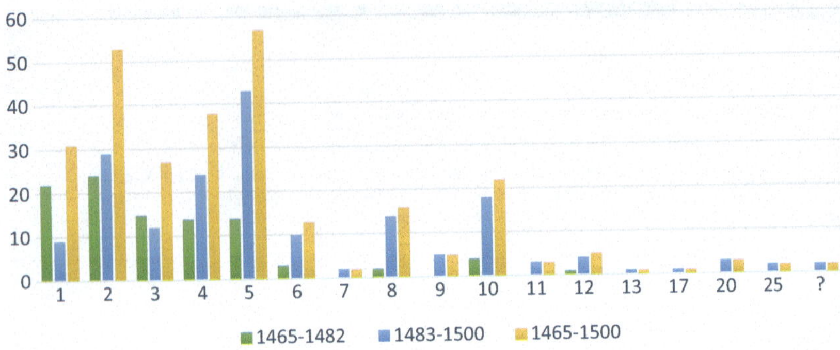


**Fig. 5.3** Number of debtors per amount of *jaarkeur* terms

the personal situation of each of the debtors was taken into account and terms were based on everyone's ability to pay. This meant that, though most debts were paid off in 1–5 terms, some people were allowed 10, 12, 20 or even 25 terms (see Fig. 5.3).

Berent van Asbeeke, for example, was given 20 years to repay his 20 *hern* lb. fine in 1498. Dirck Petersz was also allowed 20 years to pay off his 50 *hern* lb. fine in 1499, though a condition was added that he would have to pay his debt immediately if he would receive an inheritance within this period. It appears, however, that Dirck's father, who stood surety, survived for another 20 years, and Dirck completed all 20 of his terms. Whether Berent van Asbeeke did as well is not clear. There is a cross in front of his name which suggests that he paid his dues, but there is only one note on a payment of 4 *hern* lb. in 1501.

In general, debts were paid off in full. The magistrates may have been flexible in agreeing terms, but they did expect the full fines to be paid. There is little evidence of discounts for the poor, for example, like there was in medieval Ghent in composition payments.[78] The amount mentioned in the *jaarkeur* register does not always fully correspond with that in the banishment register, but these discrepancies appear especially at the start of the register and may be the result of a different way of registering the remaining amount to be paid. It may be that in these cases the first payment, perhaps made on arrival, was deducted from the amount due.

[78] Van Eetveld, 'Vrouwencriminaliteit', 176. In fourteenth-century Zürich, offenders were fined if they asked for a discount from their fines. Burghartz, *Leib, Ehre und Gut*, 88–9. For a few exceptions, see note 15.

After 1482, there are virtually no more discrepancies. There is one case in which there may have been a discount, as there is a significant discrepancy between the fine and the amount paid according to the *jaarkeur*. In 1472 Willem Blijfher was banished for a wounding at night. He was twice caught in town after this, meaning that he ended up needing to pay off a 360 lb. fine. In the *jaarkeur* register we find his father Jacob and mother Geertken promising to pay his 240 lb. fine in 12 instalments. We can then follow the annual payments in the town accounts: in 1475 Jacob paid 'for his son', in 1476, 1477 and 1478 Willem paid himself, with his parents standing surety. In 1479 and 1480 Geertken paid, and from 1481 and 1486 Jacob Blijfher picked up the bill with Geertken standing surety.[79] This was not Willem's father, however, but perhaps a brother by the same name, as other sources suggest that Jacob had died by 1479.[80] One of the Jacobs had also been banished for a wounding in 1467, but there is no record of how this fine was paid off.[81] Of course, if Jacob Blijfher had been able to pay his fine in one go, he may also have paid the first 120 lb. of Willem's fine off when his son returned. If that were in fact true, there was no discount in this case either. If there was, there is no clear evidence that it was granted. Among the entries there are only two which make mention of an exoneration of debt ('remissum'). Johan Berntsz in 1492 had been given 25 terms to repay a 50 *hern* lb. fine, but it appears that even that was too much.[82] One of his guarantors paid an instalment in 1500 and another was paid by both his guarantors in 1502, but otherwise it seems his debt remained unpaid. It was not until after 1502, though, that the magistrates decided to acquit him 'ob paupertatem'. Johan Lubbertsz, a Rhine skipper, was also due a 50 *hern* lb. fine. Eight pounds were paid in cash by someone else, whereas the rest would be fulfilled in seven instalments at six pounds. The administration shows that the first five of these were met, but the last two were not, and the remainder was exonerated.[83]

The administration of the *jaarkeur* appears to have changed slightly around 1482–83. After this date there were fewer mistakes with regard to deleting the relevant entries in the banishment register. In addition, part of the entries after 1483 mention the debtors' crimes, on which their fine

[79] SR, ff. 29r, 38v, 47r, 57r, 66v, 75r, 83r, 91r, 99r, 107r, 117r, 129r.

[80] Geertken was arranging the inheritance of their father with two of her daughters in 1479 and 1480 respectively. SAK, RA, no. 75, f. 94r (24 May 1479) and f. 102v (19 January 1480).

[81] Reg, p. 109 (1467).

[82] Reg, p. 406 (1492).

[83] Reg, p. 395 (22 November 1488).

had been based. These small changes are most likely the result of a different clerk taking over the administration: from 1482 the *jaarkeur* entries are in a different hand. Around the same time, there may have been a slight alteration in policy (whether conscious or not) which is reflected in the *jaarkeur* register. This alteration was to do with the number of instalments agreed, which was on average clearly higher in the second half of the period than in the first (see Fig. 5.3). From 1465–82 there was an average of about 3.2 instalments per arrangement, where the average between 1483 and 1500 was 5.5. This can only partly be contributed to the higher average fines recorded in this register in this period (the fines repaid were on average 4 *hern* lb. higher in the second half of the period).[84] Lower annual payments were a more significant factor. Between 1465 and 1482 the average payment per year was just over 11 *hern* lb., whereas that between 1483 and 1500 was c. 7.5 *hern* lb. Whether this was because the debtors had less money available to them towards the end of the century or because the council became more lenient when arranging terms, as said either consciously or not, remains unclear. It is notable that there were also nearly twice as many offenders seeking to arrange to pay in terms in the second period. As has been pointed out before, there was slight economic decline in the fifteenth century, and some Kampen officials were receiving less pay later in the fifteenth century than before, but it is unclear whether these numbers can have anything to do with that.[85]

There are not many other towns where the practice of payment of fines in instalments has been analysed, most likely because of a lack of sources. Another town which does also boast such an administration is Konstanz. The magistrates there were also flexible in their dealings with debtors, though most fines appear to have been paid much more quickly than they were in Kampen. Of 384 fines, 219 were paid within a year, whereas in Kampen debtors paid in annual instalments, making it much more unusual for anyone to pay off a debt within a year. Like in Kampen, though, the Konstanz magistrates looked at individual cases and did allow offenders to take as long as they needed to redeem their fines and were not too strict when it came to paying on time.[86] There is some evidence that in Konstanz

[84] In the period 1465–82, the average fine that was repaid was 26.53 *hern* lb.; in the period 1483–1500 it was 30.5 *hern* lb.

[85] For example, earlier in the century the 'stokmeester' received 19½ *hern* lb. per annum, later only 15 *hern* lb. LD, f. 170r (1432; 1451), f. 218v (1468; 1483). See also SR, f. 179v: Berent de stokmeister xv lb. (1490).

[86] Schuster, *Stadt vor Gericht*, 233–4; Schuster, 'The age of debt?', 46–7.

the magistrates sometimes renegotiated terms with debtors and asked for pledges, something which cannot be verified with regard to Kampen. Schuster argues that through 'patience, meticulousness, force and persistence' the Konstanz magistrates succeeded in claiming most of the fines due to them: at least 75 per cent was paid off in full, whereas no more than 10 per cent did not pay anything at all.[87] The latter were mainly those that fled or left the city.[88]

In Kampen, too, a large majority of debtors who chose to return to or remain in town redeemed their fines in full. Only 12 of 316 entries (3.8 per cent) were not deleted. We can therefore conclude that its magistrates also implemented a most successful system to entice its debtors to pay. In Konstanz the council ensured payment in various ways. First of all, a debtor's oath to pay entailed that a failure to pay could, in principle, result in coercive measures (*Zwangsverfahren*) being initiated against the debtor, which could eventually lead to a loss of life and goods on charges of oath breaking. The use of pledges and guarantors also provided important incentives to pay, both for the debtors and for their guarantors. Finally, Schuster argues, the system also functioned because the town magistrates treated their debtors with patience and trust.[89] In Kampen there is no specific evidence of oaths being sworn by debtors when they arranged the payment of their fines, but the fact of the administration of the arrangements does suggest a binding contract between city and offender. The other factors mentioned by Schuster are valid for Kampen too.

A relation of debt automatically created a bond between creditor and debtor, in this case between the magistrates and the offender.[90] This means that an arrangement with a higher number of instalments may have had a positive effect on their relationship: the offender may have felt bound by the debt to improve his or her behaviour for the time being. Despite this potential effect, there are a few cases in which people offended again while still paying off a debt. In 1494, for example, wagoner Evert Twenth was banished for a wounding at night in the town's bath house. He was soon able to negotiate his return, with his father, brother and two others as guarantors, and his horses and wagon as surety. He arranged to pay his 50

[87] 'Geduld, Sorgfalt, Nachdruck und Hartnäckigkeit': Schuster, *Stadt vor Gericht*, 243; ibid., 243–5.

[88] Ibid., 246.

[89] Ibid., 255–6.

[90] Schuster, 'The age of debt?', 41, 45.

*hern* lb. in eight instalments. But after having paid three instalments in 1494, 1495 and 1496, his payments stalled. The reason was that Twenth had committed another wounding, this time during the day on one of the dykes, and he was banished again. Despite his previous outstanding debt, and his lowly profession, Twenth was able to negotiate a second return in 1498. Again, eight terms were agreed upon and his brother and another man stood surety. This second fine, of 25 *hern* lb., appears to have been paid off in full, but the first one seems not to have been. One more payment was registered in 1501, but a note 'dubium' was added in the margin, suggesting that the scribe was not entirely certain whether the debt was paid off, or not.[91]

A similar case was that of Henrick Scherynck who was convicted twice in the same year: first for trying to stab someone with a knife and allowing dice games to be played in his house. He arranged to pay for the fines, 22½ *hern* lb. in total, on conviction in 1497. He paid the first instalment before he was banished for a wounding at night later in the same year. He arranged for the payment of this fine in 20 instalments and paid off this fine, but he too appears to have missed some of the payments to redeem the first fine and this remained undeleted.[92] Unfortunately, we do not have the town accounts for these years, so it is not possible to check these to confirm whether or not the first debts in these cases were paid off or not. It would also have been interesting to see how these two simultaneous debts were registered. It may be that the amounts were added up and that actually both were paid off at the same time.

These two examples are useful in that they show that the magistrates were amenable to even allowing people that were already in debt, and twice banished for the non-payment of a fine to negotiate a financial arrangement and a return to Kampen, without any apparent further repercussions. Other cases also show that banishments for the non-payment of a fine did not lead to a decrease in people's ability to act as respectable members of the community. For example, Johan Borre had been banished in 1465 with two others for a wounding by day. He negotiated his return in 1466. One of his companions, Henric Palmer, also came back to Kampen, but not until 1478.[93] Borre was one of the people standing surety for him at that time. In addition, Borre can be found as a debtor

[91] Reg, pp. 145 (1494), 150 (1497), 410 (1494), 416 (1498).
[92] Reg, pp. 151 (1497), 414 (1497), 418 (1498).
[93] Reg, pp. 105 (1465), 373 (1466); p. 382 (1478).

and creditor in other sources.[94] Not every offender can be found in other sources. This may be because they had names that are too non-specific, or because they had a social position which restricted their financial and legal activities. A servant will have left behind less footprints in the sources than their master.

An unusual case is that of Henric van Leyden. Henric had been banished in 1465 for a wounding and renegotiated his return in the same year. Three of his guarantors were dyers, so he may have been a dyer himself. The debt appears to have been paid off in full in five instalments, the final payment probably taking place in 1470.[95] But in the same year that Van Leyden had been banished and returned, in May, Henric van Leyden was also convicted of counterfeiting coins. He swore an *oervede* oath, was branded on his cheek and banished at a distance of five miles.[96] However, in 1466 a Henric van Leyden was wounded, and a man by the same name appears regularly in the sources in the 1470s.[97] A servant of his was, moreover, wounded in 1475.[98]A likely explanation would be that there are in fact two men by the same name. But there is no differentiation added to the names anywhere suggesting that they were indeed different men. If there was indeed only one man, this would suggest that he was redeemed by the magistrates despite his branding and banishment for life, and able to return to being a well-functioning member of society.

An important difference between legal practice in Konstanz and Kampen is that in more than half of Konstanz cases the punishment meted out by the court was transferred into another. Fines in particular were paid off through labour, or banishments and jail sentences were changed into fines or labour for the city (mainly working for the town building master), but other exchanges took place as well.[99] Conversely, in Kampen the non-payment of fines resulted in banishment, but in most cases this was not an alternative penalty.[100] In Konstanz offenders tried to prevent being exiled if they could, but Kampen offenders did not have the option of working

[94] SAK, RA, no. 75, f. 25r (26 May 1475) and f. 126v (12 October 1481).

[95] Reg, p. 104 (1465), p. 372 (1465).

[96] Reg, p. 8 (1465).

[97] For example, SAK, RA, no. 75, f. 37v (27 March 1476); Reg, p. 107 (1466), SR, f. 32r (1475).

[98] Reg, p. 122.

[99] Schuster, *Stadt vor Gericht*, 247.

[100] For possible exceptions, see Chap. 4.

off their debts through labour. As a result, more people were banished from Kampen each year than from Konstanz.[101]

Considering the evidence, it appears that the town magistrates did not generally banish offenders unable to pay their fines to get rid of them altogether. They showed themselves amenable in allowing debtors to pay off their debts in as many yearly instalments as necessary. They appeared to have made no difference in their treatment of those who had fled justice, those who had failed to pay their fine and had been banished, and those who arranged for a payment plan immediately. This practice ensured that Kampen inhabitants who had families, relations and an occupation within the town could remain, and were able to earn an income by continuing to work. In addition, they could use their personal networks to generate money. The magistrates did insist on payment, though, and if none was forthcoming, unless in very extraordinary circumstances, people were ousted from the community. On the other hand, there is no evidence that any of the debtors who had already arranged to pay back their debts were banished again or declared an exile when they failed to meet these payments. There are 12 debtors in the *jaarkeur* register whose entries were not deleted and for whom at least some of the payments were not indicated as having been made. As noted above, four of these were by men who had sworn an oath. We also have some of the relevant town accounts which include comments on the non-payment of these instalments, such as 'restis de multis terminis' or 'restis noch van voele jaire'. After about ten years of non-payment the magistrates appear to have given up, as the debtors then generally disappear from the record. A number of them were not originally from Kampen, so they may simply never have returned to Kampen for whatever reason, or only irregularly (some did do some of the payments). Of others it is unclear what happened. But there is no evidence that any of the 12 were declared banished again.

Those unable to pay their fines who did not have strong enough connections to the town and its community to want to make an effort to make any payments did most likely not come back to Kampen, or they were not allowed to return. It is quite possible that the fines for violent offences

[101] In Konstanz between 1444 and 1453, 50 offenders (so on average five a year) were either banished or imprisoned (33 as a sole punishment, 13 in addition to a fine and 4 in addition to labour). These are punishments that were actually undertaken, and this number disregards any banishments meted out for more serious crimes. Schuster, *Stadt vor Gericht*, 247 (table). The population of both towns is considered to have been approximately the same in the fifteenth century: 6–8000.

were deliberately high so the town could easily rid itself of undesirables if they committed an offence, and were unwilling or unable to redeem themselves for their crime. The town magistrates were probably happy to be rid of such people, who had broken the law, often by conducting violent offences, had no particular bonds to the city and had nothing to contribute financially. In addition, their failure to pay the fine, and, as such, their debt to society, may also have been considered in the context of their morality. In medieval society, debt and morality were considered to be linked, and the failure to pay a debt was considered to be deserving of punishment in itself. The question whether the same can be said for fines is discussed in the final section of this chapter.

## Debt, Fines and Morality

Medieval man was linked to others through many credit relations, especially in towns. Such relations were put under strain when individuals failed to pay their debts, and solutions were sought in ecclesiastical and civil regulations for the enforcement of minor credit. Initially, it was the church courts which provided such solutions, and creditors used canonical procedures to pressurise debtors into paying. The reason why church lawyers and courts felt such issues were part of their remit was that unpaid debts were considered as breaches of faith between two Christians who had entered into an agreement. The obligation to repay a debt was seen as sacred. So, commerce was viewed as an intricate part of a Christian moral society which was based on trust and charity. A failure to pay damaged this trust and it revealed a lack of charity on the part of the debtor. It was the duty of Christians to correct the sin of defaulting debtors.[102]

The remedy offered by the church was excommunication for debt. This excommunication acted as a coercive measure to get Christian debtors to pay, especially concerning privately recorded debts and sales on credit. Its use in much of Europe from the thirteenth to the sixteenth centuries suggests that it was considered to be useful by creditors. This may partly be because, until the end of the middle ages, civil courts were unwilling or unable to provide similarly effective, and relatively cheap, solutions. By the fifteenth century, increasingly more elite observers criticised the use of excommunication for debt. At the same time, secular courts contested the ecclesiastical jurisdiction over a number of questions, including those of

[102] Lange, *Excommunication for Debt*, 4, 41, 46.

contract and credit.[103] Tyler Lange has concluded that in the diocese of Utrecht, to which Kampen belonged, civil courts may have developed secular solutions 'in the absence of an adequate supply of ecclesiastical justice'.[104] Elsewhere, such as in England and the Italian city states, imprisonment for debt was introduced as an alternative to excommunication already in the fourteenth century.[105]

Even if excommunication for debt may have been uncommon in the Utrecht diocese, the excommunication and punishment of defaulting on debts in general were a clear indication of the strong links between debt and morality. As Lange has stated 'excommunication for debt confirmed that credit was at once a moral, social and economic quantity that reflected the state of one's soul, one's social status and one's economic position'.[106] Ireland has called debt a 'form of sin or social offence which merited punishment'.[107] Of course, one can question to what extent issues of morality influenced creditors, who may mainly have been looking for an efficient remedy for their practical problems concerning minor credit. Such remedies were, for example, offered by the charter of the town of Haarlem from 1245, where defaulting debtors could be held in town arrest for two weeks before being handed over to their creditors. These were then allowed to keep their debtors in custody until arrangements had been met for the payment of the debt.[108]

In Kampen, there are no specific by-laws in the *Boeck van Rechte* or the *Gulden Boeck* concerning debt. There is evidence of cases being settled in court concerning debt, such as in the *Liber Causarum*, and there are witness testimonies in the *Liber Testium* concerning sales and debts resulting from them.[109] But there is no evidence from legal practice of banishment being used in cases of private debt, although, as we have seen, some people were banished for defaulting on debts to the city (see Chap. 2). As such, we do not get a clear sense of the perceptions of debt in general on the part of the Kampen magistrates or the population.

[103] Ibid., 4, 29, 41, 73–5, 210. See also Chap. 4.

[104] Lange, *Excommunication for Debt*, 212.

[105] See Ireland, 'Theory and Practice'; Geltner, *The Medieval Prison*.

[106] Lange, *Excommunication for Debt*, 66.

[107] Ireland, 'Theory and Practice', 57.

[108] Dijkman, 'Debt litigation', 229.

[109] For example, LC, f. 3r (1475); LT, f. 184r (1491). For the *Liber Testium* as a source for financial transactions in medieval Kampen, see also Frankot, 'Legal business outside the courts'.

We can ask to what extent the non-payment of fines was considered to be similar to defaulting on debts. When the by-law laying down fines for illegal returns to the city after a banishment differentiates between those ousted for failing to pay a fine and debtors, this suggests that the two were considered to be related. But seeing that debtors only had to pay half the fine compared to the individuals who did not pay their fines, it seems the latter were judged more harshly. Of course, this may be because of the combination of their fineable offence and the fact that they did not pay, whereas the debtors were only guilty of defaulting on their payment. Both were able, in principle, to redeem themselves quite simply by paying their dues. There were no further obvious consequences, though it may be that the magistrates would be wary of renting out town properties again to those who had defaulted on payments in the past. From the language used in the legal records, we get no sense of any links between debt and morality, as we do concerning certain behaviour in the final quarter of the fifteenth century (see Chap. 4). This does not mean that such links did not exist, as the banishment records are very concise, but that there simply is no record of it.

At the same time, banishment was a serious measure that was otherwise meted out to sexual offenders in particular. This in itself might indicate that the magistrates did consider a failure to pay a fine in the context of a person's morality. As members of the town community, people had a responsibility to uphold the law. As suggested in Chap. 4, a failure to do so, and then not facing the consequences by paying a fine, could be considered a breach of faith. Interesting in this context is the fact that some offenders appear to have arranged terms for payment directly following their trial, whereas others apparently had not. It may be that the magistrates expected people to come forward themselves rather than them offering a financial arrangement as a possibility to everyone. If an offender did not take responsibility for paying off their fine, this was their own fault and they should bear the consequence, and this consequence was exile.

In conclusion, redemption after a banishment was possible for most offenders, though the route to redemption might have varied. Individuals who had been banished outright could negotiate a return after a certain amount of time unless they had been cast out permanently. It is unclear, though, how it was decided when someone could come back. This may have depended on the culprit's reputation, status and crime, but also perhaps on the efforts of their social network. It appears that a banishment did not have negative repercussions on someone's ability to function normally after their return. The offence was apparently amended through the banishment. To those banished for failing to pay a fine, redemption could be effected by arranging the payment of the amount due. Only about a third of outcasts chose this route; the rest remained banished. Both groups included different social classes. The Kampen magistrates appear to have been happy to set up financial arrangements and showed themselves flexible in offering terms. Fines generally needed to be paid off in full, but exceptions were made, and no one was banished again when terms remained unpaid. But for the most part offenders paid their dues in full and an effective system to guarantee payments appears to have been in place. Vital to the reintegration of these outcasts were their relatives and friends, who stood surety and probably played an important role in early negotiations for a return. Although the magistrates appeared to have been happy to allow people to return, there is some evidence that suggests that they did consider it the responsibility of the offenders to come forward to make arrangements. This may have been considered part of the culprit's moral duty as a public debtor. There is no specific evidence that the non-payment of fines was seen as a moral failure, but it is perhaps telling that defaulters were banished when banishment as a punishment was mostly meted out to those displaying immoral behaviour.

# Conclusion

*Abstract*
The conclusion establishes what the various forms of banishment and the redemption of exiles can tell us about the values of late medieval urban society concerning morally acceptable behaviour.

When Derick Sael and his family appeared before the court in November 1478, their sentence suggested that certain behaviours were not tolerated in late medieval Kampen. They ended up receiving a warning, but others were banished for offences that ranged from extensive misbehaviour and adultery to vagabondage and small theft. A majority of exiles, however, were ousted because they were unable or unwilling to pay fines which were mostly meted out for violent offences. This book has aimed to establish what the various forms of banishment and the redemption of exiles can tell us about the values of late medieval urban society concerning morally acceptable behaviour.

The majority of offenders that were banished, or that were threatened with banishment, had been charged with sexual offences, such as adultery and facilitating illegal sexual acts, or general misbehaviour. Individuals charged with domestic violence, mostly men, were generally given warnings, and, overall, women were more regularly banished for sexual offences than men. There was a clear increase in the banishment of women for sexual offences in the final quarter of the fifteenth century. It is also apparent from the language used in the records that there was an increasing



E. Frankot, *Banishment in the Late Medieval Eastern Netherlands*,
https://doi.org/10.1007/978-3-030-88867-1

focus on morality in the final decades of the 1400s. This increase can be considered part of an urban morality movement that is also recognisable elsewhere in Europe, and the findings for Kampen concerning the treatment of individuals charged with immoral behaviour probably have a wider validity.

It is likely that the growing focus on morality was initiated by certain groups of the Kampen population who increasingly took offence when confronted with the perceived immoral acts of their neighbours, no doubt (further) inspired by Brugman's preaching. When their own efforts to intervene had been unsuccessful, they increasingly denounced these neighbours to the authorities, thus communicating to the magistrates and the rest of the population the boundaries of acceptable behaviour. In the third quarter of the fifteenth century the magistrates responded with additional by-laws regulating adultery and procuring, thus confirming the boundaries set by the denouncers, while at the same time sentencing in a still relatively mild manner. In the final quarter, however, an increasing number of banishment sentences, particularly of women, suggests that the magistrates themselves also became increasingly convinced of the need to police and punish immoral behaviour.

Even though people were banished for failing to pay a fine which generally resulted from acts of violence, violence itself was not considered morally offensive. Medieval urban society was characterised by a relatively high willingness to use violence, though, generally, confrontations occurred according to a ritualistic sequence of events which prevented excess. Nonetheless, the number of conflicts in Kampen which ended in bloodshed makes one question how effective such rituals were there. In certain circumstances, violence was considered to be an acceptable response. At the same time, magistrates sought to maintain a peaceful town by trying to restrict private violence as much as possible. The main measure they could employ to achieve this was to fine offenders. It was only when offenders failed to pay a fine, and as such failed to take responsibility to amend their acts, that people were banished. It is likely that this failure was considered in the context of a person's morality. Defaulting on debts more generally was seen as a sin, damaging the trust between Christians. The banishment of defaulting public debtors in Kampen was likely at least partly considered in this fashion, though the magistrates may also have had pragmatic motives in ridding the town of undesirables.

Many exiles were eventually allowed to re-join the town community. Culprits who had been banished outright may have been considered to have redeemed themselves after they had spent a certain amount of time away. Defaulting debtors simply had to pay the sum due, or arrange for a payment in terms. In both cases, the social network of the offenders played a vital role in negotiating with the magistrates and in providing the necessary guarantees for behaviour or payment. It is likely that the two-thirds of exiles who did not return to Kampen lacked a solid social network. There is little evidence that a banishment for any reason led to long-lasting effects on people's ability to function as full members of the town community, at least when it came to their legal and financial activities. It is virtually impossible to gain a complete picture of someone's social standing and reputation, especially if they were not active legally or financially. But it seems to have been the case that through banishment, offenders were considered to have redeemed themselves.

It is difficult to assess to what extent social status affected the banishment and redemption of offenders. People of various backgrounds ended up outside the town after failing to pay their fines, and a similarly varied group negotiated financial arrangements with the magistrates. It is likely that the richest members of the community were able to pay their fines immediately, but they too ended up before the court. It does appear to have been the case that people from outside of town ended up in custody more regularly, and it was also mostly outsiders who ended up being capitally punished. Ironically, these were often individuals who had at some point been banished from a town.

Capital, corporal and shameful punishments were mostly meted out publicly in order to display the magistrates' commitment to maintaining peace and social order. A pillory ('kaak') was erected in a public place by the town hall, though it appears to have had a mainly symbolic function, as few offenders were sentenced to standing on it. There is little evidence that banishments were accompanied by ceremony as a rule, although some offenders were, for example, flogged and banished. But most outcasts appear to have been allowed to leave of their own accord. As such, it was mostly other penal practices that served a symbolic function in the application of authority in Kampen. By the final decades of the fifteenth century, the magistrates were prepared to punish perceived immoral acts with banishments, but they appear not yet to have been willing to turn the expulsion of the offenders guilty of such acts into a spectacle. It may be that this changed in the sixteenth century, especially after the Reformation. In their maintenance of public order, the magistrates greatly depended on the support of the population. The inhabitants were expected to denounce others, to help execute banishments effectively by looking out for exiles illegally returning, and to collaborate with the magistrates in welcoming outcasts back. In Kampen this collaboration appears to have been successful in that there is little evidence of social unrest in the later middle ages. In addition, the success in setting up a fairly effective system of financial arrangements between inhabitants and magistrates suggests that trust and flexibility characterised most of their relations.

There is little evidence that Kampen suffered from the existence of an 'army of exiles' outside its walls, as opposed to some of the other towns discussed. It is difficult to offer an explanation for this. Perhaps exiles found a temporary home in one of the towns nearby, like Zwolle, or perhaps all evidence has been lost. The fact remains that there was a steady stream of two to three people per month being cast out of Kampen and it is likely that the same was the case for many other towns in the Low Countries and Germany. It would be an exaggeration to say that the countryside was awash with exiles, but they certainly formed a sizeable group about whose lives we know but very little.

# Bibliography

## Manuscript Sources

### Stadsarchief Kampen (Town Archives Kampen) [SAK]

#### Oud Archief [OA]

no. 5 *Dat Boeck van Rechte dier Stat van Campen* (1313–1416) [BvR].
no. 6 *Dat Gulden Boeck* (1329–1614) [GB].
no. 8 *Digestum Vetus* (1448–1478) [DV].
no. 11 *Liber Diversorum C* (1399–1553) [LD].
no. 242 *Digestum Novum* (1450–1567) [DN].
no. 332 *Burgerboek* (1302–1469) [BB].
no. 402 *Stedelijke Rekeningen* (town accounts) (1472–1494) [SR].

#### Rechterlijk Archief [RA]

no. 1 *Register* (1447–1578) [Reg].
no. 2 *Liber Causarum* (1475–1604) [LC].
no. 6 *Liber Testium* (1483–93) [LT].
no. 75 *Liber Recognitionum* (1474–89).
no. 76 *Liber Recognitionum* (1474–96).


E. Frankot, *Banishment in the Late Medieval Eastern Netherlands*,
https://doi.org/10.1007/978-3-030-88867-1

## Edited Primary Sources

Frankot, E., A. Havinga, C. Hawes, W. Hepburn. W. Peters, J. Armstrong, P. Astley, A. Mackillop, A.R.C. Simpson, A. Wyner, eds, *Aberdeen Registers Online* (Aberdeen 2019), www.abdn.ac.uk/aro.

*Overijsselsche Stad-, Dijk- en Markeregten, vol. I. Stadregten, eerste stuk: Boeck van Rechten der Stad Kampen, Dat Gulden Boeck* (Zwolle 1875).

## Secondary Works

Althoff, G., 'The variability of rituals in the middle ages', in: G. Althoff, J. Fried and P.J. Geary, eds, *Medieval Concepts of the Past* (Cambridge etc 2002), 71–87.

Arnade, P., and W. Prevenier, *Honor, Vengeance, and Social Trouble. Pardon Letters in the Burgundian Low Countries* (Ithaca 2015).

Benders, J.F., *Bestuursstructuur en schriftcultuur. Een analyse van de bestuurlijke verschriftelijking in Deventer tot het eind van de 15e eeuw* (Kampen 2004).

Berents, D.A., *Misdaad in de Middeleeuwen. Een onderzoek naar de criminaliteit in het laat-middeleeuwse Utrecht* (Utrecht 1976).

Berents, D.A., *Het werk van de vos. Samenleving en criminaliteit in de late middeleeuwen* (Zutphen 1985).

Blauert, A., *Das Urfehdewesen im deutschen Südwesten im Spätmittelalter und in der frühen Neuzeit* (Tübingen 2000).

Blauert, A., and G. Schwerhoff, eds, *Mit den Waffen der Justiz. Zur Kriminalitätsgeschichte des Spätmittelalters und der frühen Neuzeit* (Frankfurt am Main 1993).

Blockmans, W., and T. Neijzen, 'Functions of fiction: fighting spouses around 1500', in: W. Blockmans and A. Janse, eds, *Showing Status: Representations of Social Positions in the Late Middle Ages* (Turnhout 1999), 265–76.

Boer, D.E.H. de, and E. Frankot, 'Digestum Digitaal. Kamper verleden op de electronische snelweg', *Kamper Almanak* (2006), 33–50.

Boockmann, A., *Urfehde und ewige Gefangenschaft im mittelalterlichen Göttingen* (Göttingen 1980).

Boomgaard, J.E.A., *Misdaad en straf in Amsterdam: een onderzoek naar de strafrechtspleging van de Amsterdamse schepenbank* (Zwolle 1992).

Brakensiek, S., 'Herrschaftsvermittlung im alten Europa. Praktiken lokaler Justiz, Politik und Verwaltung im internationalen Vergleich', in: S. Brakensiek and H. Wunder, eds, *Ergebene Diener ihrer Herren? Herrschaftsvermittlung im alten Europa* (Cologne etc. 2005), 1–21.

Brand, H. and E. Frankot, 'Das Kampener Stadtbuch Digestum Vetus als Spiegel der städtischen Normierungspolitik', in: H. Brand, S. Rabeler and H. von Seggern, eds, *Gelebte Normen im urbanen Raum? Zur sozial- und kulturge-*

*schichtlichen Analyse rechtlicher Quellen in Städten des Hanseraums (13. bis 16. Jahrhunderts)* (Hilversum 2014), 45–61.

Brockdorf, C. von, 'Die Strafe des Stadverweises im Spätmittelalter', in: I. Hülpes and F. Klaes, eds, *Die Stadt des Mittelalters an der Schwelle zur Frühen Neuzeit. Beiträge des interdisziplären (Post-)Doc-Workshop des Trierer Zentrums für Mediävistik im November 2017)* (Mittelalter. Interdisziplinäre Forschung und Rezeptionsgeschichte, Beihefte 1, 2018), 42–57.

Brundage, J., 'Prostitution in the medieval canon law', *Signs* 1 (1976), 825–45.

Burghartz, S., *Leib, Ehre und Gut. Delinquenz in Zürich Ende des 14. Jahrhunderts* (Zürich 1990).

Caenegem, R.C. van, *Geschiedenis van het strafrecht in Vlaanderen van de XIe tot de XIVe eeuw* (Brussels 1954).

Carlier, M., *Kinderen van der minne? Bastaarden in het vijftiende-eeuwse Vlaanderen* (Brussel 2001).

Carlier, M., and Stabel, P., 'Questions de moralité dans les villes de la Flandre au bas Moyen Âge: sexualité et activité legislative urbaine (bans échevinaux et statuts de métiers)', in: J.-M. Cauchies and E. Bousmar, eds, *'Faire bans, edictz et statuz'. Légiférer dans la ville médiévale. Sources, objets et acteurs de l'activité législative communale en occident, ca. 1200–1550* (Brussels 2001), 241–62.

Carrell, H., 'The ideology of punishment in late medieval English towns', *Social History* 34 (2009), 301–20.

Cattelona, Georg'ann, 'Control and collaboration: the role of women in regulating female sexual behavior in early modern Marseille', *French Historical Studies* 18 (1993), 13–33.

Cohen, E., 'Violence control in late medieval France. The social transformation of the Asseurement', *Legal History Review* 51 (1983), 111–22.

Cohen, E., *The Crossroads of Justice. Law and Culture in late medieval France* (Leiden 1993).

Coy, J.P., 'Beggars at the gates: Banishment and exclusion in sixteenth-century Ulm', *The Sixteenth Century Journal* 39 (2008), 619–38.

Coy, J.P., *Strangers and Misfits: Banishment, social control, and authority in Early Modern Germany* (Leiden 2008).

Crawford, K., *European Sexualities, 1400–1800* (Cambridge 2007).

Dean, T., *Crime in Medieval Europe* (Harlow etc. 2001).

Dean, T., *Crime and Justice in Late Medieval Italy* (Cambridge 2007).

Dijkman, J., 'Debt litigation in medieval Holland', in: D. Ma and J. Luiten van Zanden, eds, *Law and Long-Term Economic Change: A Eurasian Perspective* (Stanford 2011), 221–43.

Dupont, G., *Maagdenverleidsters, hoeren en speculanten: prostitutie in Brugge tijdens de Bourgondische periode (1385–1515)* (Bruges 1996).

Ewan, E., 'Disorderly Damsels? Women and interpersonal violence in Pre-Reformation Scotland', *Scottish Historical Review* 89 (2010), 153–71.

Ewan, E., '"Tongue you lied": The role of the tongue in rituals of public penance in late medieval Scotland', in: E.D. Craun, ed., *The Hands of the Tongue: essays on deviant speech* (Kalamazoo 2007), 115–36.

Ewan, E., 'Crossing borders and boundaries: the use of banishment in sixteenth-century Scottish towns', in: S.M. Butler and K.J. Kesselring, eds, *Crossing Borders: boundaries and margins in medieval an early modern Britain* (Leiden and Boston 2018), 237–57.

Frankot, E., *'Of Laws of Ships and Shipmen'. Medieval Maritime Law and its Practice in Urban Northern Europe* (Edinburgh 2012).

Frankot, E., 'Legal business outside the courts: Private and public houses as spaces of law in the fifteenth century', in: J.W. Armstrong and E. Frankot, eds, *Cultures of Law in Urban Northern Europe: Scotland and its Neighbours c.1350–c.1650* (London and New York 2020), 173–91.

Gauvard, C., *'De grace especial': Crime, état et société en France* (Paris 1991).

Geltner, G., *The Medieval Prison. A Social History* (Princeton 2008).

Geltner, G., *Flogging Others: Corporal Punishment and Cultural Identity from Antiquity to the Present* (Amsterdam 2015).

Glaudemans, C., *Om die wrake wille. Eigenrichting, vete en verzoening in laat-middeleeuws Holland en Zeeland* (Hilversum 2004).

Grooten, J., 'Kampen an der IJssel', in: J. Bräcker, V. Henn and R. Postel, eds, *Die Hanse – Lebenswirklichkeit und Mythos* (3rd edition, Lübeck 1999), 299–301.

Hamel, S., 'Bannis et bannissement à Saint-Quentin aux derniers siècles du Moyen Âge', *Hypothèses* 1 (2002), 123–33.

Hanawalt, B.A., '"Good governance" in the medieval and early modern context', *The Journal of British Studies* 37 (1998), 246–57.

Hanawalt, B.A., '"Of Good and Ill Repute": The limits of community tolerance', in: *'Of Good and Ill Repute'. Gender and Social Culture in Medieval England* (New York 1998), 1–17.

Hanawalt, B.A., 'Rituals of inclusion and exclusion: Hierarchy and marginalization in medieval London', in: *'Of Good and Ill Repute'*, 18–34.

Harrington, J.F., *The Faithful Executioner. Life and Death in the sixteenth century* (London 2013).

Hawes, C., 'The urban community in fifteenth-century Scotland: Language, law and political practice', *Urban History* 44 (2016) ('special section: Communities, courts and Scottish towns', J.W. Armstrong and A. Mackillop, eds), 365–80.

Helmholz, R.H., 'Harboring sexual offenders: ecclesiastical courts and controlling misbehavior', *The Journal of British Studies* 37 (1998), 258–68.

Herwaarden, J. van, *Opgelegde bedevaarten Een studie over de praktijk van opleggen van bedevaarten (met name in de stedelijke rechtspraak) in de Nederlanden gedurende de late middeleeuwen (ca. 1300 – ca. 1500)* (Assen and Amsterdam 1978).

Hoffmann, C.A., 'Der Stadtverweis als Sanktionsmittel in der Reichstadt Augsburg zu Beginn der Neuzeit', in: H. Schlosser and D. Willoweit, eds, *Neue Wege strafrechtsgeschichtlicher Forschung* (Cologne etc 1999), 193–237.

Houts, E. van, 'Preface', in: Napran and van Houts, eds, *Exile in the Middle Ages*, xi–xii.

Houts, E. van, 'The vocabulary of exile and outlawry in the North Sea area around the first millennium', in: Napran and van Houts, eds, *Exile in the Middle Ages*, 13–28.

Huart, S., 'Maintenir la paix dans la communauté et affirmer l'identité urbaine: bannis et bannissement à Valenciennes au XIVe siècle', *Questes: bulletin des jeunes chercheurs médiévistes* (2016), 85–101, https://hal.archives-ouvertes.fr/hal-01378650.

Ireland, R.W., 'Theory and practice within the medieval English prison', *The American Journal of Legal History*, 31 (1987), 57–62.

Jacob, R., 'Bannissement et rite de la langue tirée au Moyen Âge: Du lien des lois et de sa rupture', *Annales. Histoire, sciences sociales* 55 (2000), 1039–79.

Jeziorski, P.A., 'Die Strafe der Ausweisung aus der Stadt im Licht der preussischen Verfestungsbücher (14.-15. Jahrhundert)', in: Brand, Rabeler, Von Seggern, eds, *Gelebte Normen*, 29–44.

Kossmann-Putto, J.A., *Kamper schepenacten 1316–1354* (Zwolle 1955).

Kossmann-Putto, J.A., 'Stadsbestuur van Kampen in de middeleeuwen', in: idem, *Over middeleeuwse geschiedenis. Elf opstellen* (Utrecht 2009), 57–73.

Laitinen, R., 'Banishment, urban community and judicial practice: thieves in mid-17th-century Turku', *Scandinavian Journal of History* 38 (2013), 549–67.

Lange, T., *Excommunication for Debt in Late Medieval France: The Business of Salvation* (Cambridge and New York 2016).

Lansing, C., 'Gender and civic authority: Sexual control in a medieval Italian town', *Journal of Social History* 31 (1997), 33–59.

Lansing, C., *Passion and Order. Restraint of grief in the medieval Italian communes* (Ithaca and London 2008).

Lettinck, N., *Praten als Brugman. De wereld van een Nederlandse volksprediger aan het einde van de middeleeuwen* (Hilversum 1999).

Lipscomb, S., *Voices of Nîmes. Women, Sex, and Marriage in Reformation Languedoc* (Oxford 2019).

McIntosh, M.K., 'Finding language for misconduct. Jurors in fifteenth-century local courts', in: B.A. Hanawalt and D. Wallace, eds, *Bodies and Disciplines: the intersection of literature and history in fifteenth-century England* (Minneapolis 1996), 87–122.

Marchal, G.P., '"Von der Stadt" und bis ins "Pfefferland". Städtische Raum- und Grenzvorstellingen in Urfehden und Verbanningsurteilen oberrheinischer und schweizerischer Städte', in: G.P. Marchal, ed., *Grenzen und Raumvorstellungen*

*(11.-20. Jh.)/Frontières et conceptions de l'espace (11e-20e siècles)* (Zürich 1996), 225–63.

Maurer, H., 'Erzwungene Ferne. Zur räumlichen Dimension der Stadtverweisung im Spätmittelalter', in: Marchal, ed., *Grenzen und Raumvorstellungen*, 199–224.

Müller, M., *Misdaad en straf in een Hollandse stad: Haarlem, 1245–1615* (Hilversum 2017).

Napran, L., 'Introduction: Exile in context', in: Napran and van Houts, eds, *Exile in the Middle Ages*, 1–9.

Napran, L., and E. van Houts, eds, *Exile in the Middle Ages. Selected Proceedings from the International Medieval Congress, University of Leeds, 8–11 July 2002* (Turnhout 2004).

Næss, H.E., and E. Österberg, 'Sanctions, agreements, sufferings', in: E. Österberg and S.B. Sogner, eds, *People Meet the Law: Control and Conflict-Handling in the Courts. The Nordic Countries in the Post-Reformation and Pre-Industrial Period* (Oslo 2000), 140–66.

Prak, M., *Citizens without Nations. Urban Citizenship in Europe and the World c. 1000–1789* (Cambridge 2018).

Pythian-Adams, C.V., 'Rituals of personal confrontation in late medieval England', *Bulletin of the John Rylands Library* 73 (1991), 65–90.

Robijn, V., *Het recht van een vrije Friese stad. De stadboeken van Bolsward (1455–1479)* (Hilversum 2005).

Schilder, K., *Digestum Vetus 1448–1478 (Kamper genealogische en historische bronnen deel 3)* (Kampen 1983).

Schuster, P., *Stadt vor Gericht. Recht und Alltag im spätmittelalterlichen Konstanz* (Paderborn 2000).

Schuster, P., 'The age of debt? Private Schulden in der spätmittelalterlichen Gesellschaft', in: G.B. Clemens, ed., *Schuldenlast und Schuldenwert. Kreditnetzwerke in der europäischen Geschichte 1300–1900* (Trier 2008), 37–52.

Schuster, P., 'Hinaus oder ins Frauenhaus. Weibliche sexualität und gesellschaftliche Kontrolle an der Wende vom Mittelalter zur Neuzeit', in: Blauert and Schwerhoff, eds, *Mit den Waffen der Justiz*, 17–31.

Schwerhoff, G., 'Verordnete Schande? Spätmittelalterliche und frühneuzeitliche Ehrenstrafen zwischen Rechtsakt und sozialer Sanktion', in: Blauert and Schwerhoff, eds, *Mit den Waffen der Justiz*, 158–88.

Smail, D.L., *The Consumption of Justice. Emotions, Publicity, and Legal Culture in Marseille, 1264–1423* (Ithaca 2003).

Snijder, C.R.H., 'Vijftiende- en zestiende-eeuwse scherprechters te Kampen', *De Nederlandsche Leeuw* 136 (2019), 97–112.

Tamboer, A., and Van Vlisteren, V., 'Celtic Bugle, Roman lituus, or medieval ban horn? An evaluation of cast bronze horns with an upturned bell', in: E. Hickman, ed., *Music Archaeology in Context* (Rahden 2006), 221–36.

Tamse, C.A., 'Bijdrage tot de economische geschiedenis van Kampen in de Middeleeuwen en de XVIe eeuw', *Kamper Almanak* (1963–64), 204–79.

Tyler, J., 'Refugees and Reform: banishment and exile in early modern Augsburg', in: R.J. Bast and A.C. Gow, eds, *Continuity and Change: the harvest of late medieval and Reformation History* (Leiden 2000), 77–97.

Vanhemelryck, F., *Misdadigers tussen recht en beul, 1400–1800* (Antwerp and Amsterdam 1984).

Vliet, L. van, 'Zeventiende-eeuwse Kamper Scherprechters', *Kamper Almanak* (2006), 81–101.

Vlis, D. van der, 'De bevolking van Kampen van het begin der vijftiende tot het begin der twintigste eeuw', *Verslagen en mededelingen van de Vereeniging tot beoefening van Overijsselsch regt en geschiedenis* 89 (1974), 1–36.

Weststrate, J., *In het kielzog van moderne markten. Handel en scheepvaart op de Rijn, Waal en IJssel, ca. 1360–1560* (Hilversum 2008).

Zaremska, H., *Les bannis au Moyen Âge* (Paris 1996).

## Unpublished Theses

Eetveld, K. van, 'Vrouwencriminaliteit in Gent tijdens de Bourgondische Period (1385–1515)' (unpublished Licentiaat thesis, University of Ghent, 2007).

De Win, P., 'De schandstraffen in België van de middeleeuwen tot de 19e eeuw. Een rechtshistorische en rechtsarcheologische studie' (unpublished PhD thesis, University of Ghent, 1989).

# INDEX[1]



[1] Note: Page numbers followed by 'n' refer to notes.


E. Frankot, *Banishment in the Late Medieval Eastern Netherlands*,
https://doi.org/10.1007/978-3-030-88867-1

The manufacturer's authorised representative in the EU is Springer Nature Customer Service Centre GmbH, Europaplatz 3, 69115 Heidelberg, Germany. If you have any concerns regarding our products, please contact ProductSafety@springernature.com

Printed and bound by CPI Group (UK) Ltd, Croydon, CR0 4YY

22/09/2026

02221063-0008